Living a Life that
Reflects Christ

A STUDY OF THE BOOK OF COLOSSIANS

ELIZABETH B MAHUSAY

AUTHOR ACADEMY elite

Mirror Image
Living a Life That Reflects Christ

Cover Design: Virtually Possible Designs
Photography: FREDSHOTS Photography
Illustrator: John Rogeles
Editor: Sheri A. Bell

Printed in the United States of America

Published by Author Academy Elite
PO BOX 43
Powell, Ohio 43035
www.AuthorAcademyElite.com

ISBN 978-1-64085-823-7
Library of Congress Control Number: 2019911715

PRAISE FOR MIRROR IMAGE

As a Pastor, I'm always trying to look for new and creative ways for God's Word to come alive in people's life. In Mirror Image, Elizabeth does just that by posing some of the deepest truths from the book of Colossians in such a way that every reader can benefit. I believe everyone who reads Mirror Image will be able to better identify their blind spots and more clearly reflect the image of Christ.

John Mark Caton, PhD
Pastor
Cottonwood Creek Baptist Church

As a therapist, I see firsthand the pain women needlessly carry when they allow their self-view to be shaped by negative thinking. In *Mirror Image,* Elizabeth's thoughtful use of biblical truths, personal stories, and the "mirror" as metaphor teaches women to effectively anchor their self-esteem in the truth of God's Word. God says YOU are beautiful, Gals! Accept it, believe it, and live it to break free of the enemy's lies so you beautifully reflect Christ!

Linda Ryan-Holbeck, MS, LCSW
Urban Cottage Counseling and Coaching for Women

This Bible Study "Mirror Image" is a game changer for any girl or woman. Knowing who you are in Christ is the start of understanding yourself, your value, and your purpose. This Bible Study will grow your confidence and a healthy self-esteem based on what God says about you. I love how practical this study is. We all need to know and be reminded of the importance of our Mirror Image!

Elizabeth Draper
Entrepreneur, leadership coach, encourager, teacher,
passionate follower of Jesus, wife, mother and grand mother.

WOW! I have struggled to walk in freedom from negative self-image since birthing and raising many children. As an aging mother of seven, four of them daughters, I am always aware that my kids are observing how I speak about myself and how I view others. Elizabeth's ability to share truth, combined with her knowledge of and passion for God's word has adjusted my lens thru which I view God's creation, even my own reflection! This uniquely interactive and engaging study should be in the hands of EVERY WOMAN who desires to be victorious in this area of her life!

Kristy Sutton
Writer, speaker, wife, foster mom, forever mom, lover of strong coffee, good conversation, and dreaming gigantic dreams!
kristybsutton.com

WOW! *Mirror Image* gets to the core of where so many women, including myself, struggle in their self-image. Elizabeth's study begins with a clear Biblical understanding of who defines our true self-worth and identity, and then explores the many ways women struggle with self-image. Elizabeth beautifully expands on how we can achieve freedom from this all too common area of bondage, as she teaches us how to live in the Spirit and not our flesh.

Elizabeth Licht
Wife, mother, business owner

Our lives can look so different if we are able to know and believe what God says about us! Elizabeth's *Mirror Image* will take you on a journey into the Word of God that unpacks core truths so you can live in freedom. Prepare for transformation in how you see yourself, how you see God, and your relationships with other people.

Abigail Doust
Executive Director, Relationship Experts

Every woman, if she is honest with herself, will relate to Elizabeth's real-world and God-led truths. Most women have a negative view of themselves. Friends, this study will lead you to see yourself as God sees you.

Theresa L. Miller
Precepts Bible Study Teacher

I highly recommend reading this book because it changed how I view myself. *Mirror Image* helps women of all ages by giving Biblical answers to the self-image questions we have. Through the daily devotionals, Elizabeth highlights what it means to reflect Christ to the world. *Mirror Image* is an impactful, must read for all teenagers.

Sophie Bellew
16 years old high school student

Mirror
IMAGE

Dedication

To my husband and sons: Thank you for loving me through all the nights and early mornings of writing, for the encouragement to stay the course, and for the daily inspiration to assess my own life and the mirror image I'm projecting.

To the women of Cottonwood Creek Church: Thank you for the privilege of serving as your women's minister; for your smiles, hugs, and prayers; and for your encouragement to continue to pursue my passion for writing, speaking, and teaching. Thank you for the opportunity to see life through your eyes, to deepen my perspective, and to grow my mission for encouraging women through the study of God's Word.

To my Social Media Tribe: Thank you for your support through sharing content, watching videos, and offering your perspective on mirrors and what they mean in your lives. Many of your quotes, which so inspired me throughout the writing process, are found within the pages of this study. Thank you!

CONTENTS

A NOTE FROM ELIZABETH

The book of Colossians is rich with truth. Truth that I desperately need, if I am to show up as my authentic self. Too often I am wooed by our smoke-and-mirrors world to project a false, "I've got it all together" reflection.

But the tension of wanting to be real, while also hiding my fears, doubts, and weaknesses, is exhausting. Ladies, we aren't meant to live like this! Here's the thing: too many of us are trying to be something God hasn't asked us to be perfect.

Worse, when we try to reach perfection by devising man-made rules and schemes, just as false teachers tried to implement in Jesus' day, we get even further from the simple truths God has provided for our daily living.

Sure, we all want to appear successful. But why are we allowing society to determine our standard of success, rather than standing firm on how God defines it?

Why do we care so much about mirroring the Joneses—and the Kardashians—and so little about reflecting Jesus? And why, for that matter, do we spend so much time gazing into mirrors to define our self-image?

I'll admit that being married to a photographer keeps my physical reflection top of mind. My husband, Fred, loves to take photos of me, and has been doing so for 20+ years. So I am only too keenly aware of every new wrinkle and the occasional gray hair. If I am not careful, I can really go dark if I compare my appearance to that of others, and judge myself to be lacking.

My tendency to do that got me thinking. On my blog, I asked my readers to note their own thoughts about mirrors and reflections and self-image. Their responses, which I share with you throughout this study guide, prompted me to focus on what God says about us in the Book of Colossians. I use mirrors as a metaphor for how we individually decide to show up in the world.

This 6-week study is designed to cultivate a desire within you to live a grounded life that genuinely reflects Christ. It is my prayer that you get so anchored in who Jesus is—and who He says you are—that you choose to wholeheartedly reflect His standards, not waste your time chasing after the world's.

Our secular world is doing everything it can to dictate how we answer the question, "Who am I?" But we only find the answer in this: a committed relationship with Christ.

I am praying for you, Sisters! As we journey through Colossians together, we will come to know our Savior more intimately, embrace how deeply and securely and lovingly He holds us, and reflect His peace and joy to others. The world needs us to mirror the beauty of Jesus!

So get prepared to dive in, go deep, and cement the truth of Christ in your life. I look forward to hearing how God's Word transforms your reflections to the world!

Elizabeth

ACKNOWLEDGEMENTS

Mirror Image is a testimony to God's gracious and loving hand in my life. I do not always like what the mirror of God's Word has shown me, but I am thankful for the correction it provides.

Thank you to my three guys: Fred, the love of my life, for your love, and gentle reminders to trust God in the completion of this book. Anthony, my oldest, for the kisses on my cheek, and the Whataburger runs. Samuel, my youngest, for the joy of hearing you play the tuba, and keeping our Spring Creek BBQ connection going!

Mirror Image was first written and taught for Heart to Heart, a women's ministry of Bell Shoals Baptist Church. I am thankful for Gayle Owens helping me to write the original study guide all those years ago.

I am thankful for my mother, Betty Bennett, who has read and edited multiple iterations of this study as I've worked through the writing process.

I am incredibly grateful for Sheri A. Bell, my developmental editor. Sheri challenged me from the beginning of my writing to be personal and authentic. She is exactly what I need to ensure that I am being the mirror image that every reader holding this book also needs.

I am thankful for my trainer, Abby Pagud with Kapitol Health for keeping my body in shape, so that my mind remained sharp during the journey.

Thank you, Trish Littlejohn, for believing in me and this project so much that you were willing to help make it possible.

I am grateful for the privilege to work alongside the amazing staff of Cottonwood Creek Church. You each inspire me to press onward, grow deeper, and serve more wholeheartedly. Your prayers, constant encouragement, and partnership in ministry are a blessing in my life! I am also thankful for Meredith Jackson, my executive ministry coordinator, who checked every Scripture reference while proofreading the study.

"Mirrors always make me stop.
Sometimes I see the good, sometimes I see the flaw,
but I almost always pause, even if for a second."
—Tiffany

FULL-LENGTH FAITH

Day 1

"Mirrors always make me stop. Sometimes I see the good, sometimes I see the flaws, but I almost always pause, even if for a second."

~Tiffany

Mirrors! We women have a love/hate relationship with them, right? There are days we love what we see, and there are days we hate what we see. Like Tiffany, we are drawn to repeatedly critique our reflection. When we spy a mirror, we always take a look. *Why are we so fixated on our external appearance?*

In Genesis 1:26, God says, "Let us make man in our image, after our likeness."

Ladies, you and I are, indeed, made in God's image. But we struggle to see ourselves that way because we've gotten into the habit of basing our self-image on what we deem beautiful about our external reflection. To put it simply, we have allowed society's standard of beauty to set our self-image, rather than God's standard.

> I refer to "self-image" a lot throughout this study. So let's establish a working definition: ***Self-image is the idea one has of one's abilities, appearance, and personality.***

An important part of that definition: our reflection isn't just determined by what we see. *What we think about ourselves dramatically influences what we see.* If our thoughts are based on a skewed standard, of course we're going to see a skewed reflection!

In 2018, Today online magazine published a survey of more than 1,000 women and men.[1] The article shared that what they see in mirrors only accounts for one percent of how they view their bodies. A substantial number (88 percent!) of the women surveyed said they *compare* their body to images they see in the media. And the majority admitted they feel inferior by comparison. It sure is a challenge to see ourselves the way God intended: a daughter made in God's image. If only sin had not entered into God's creation.

Eve was perfectly at peace in her nakedness—until her fateful bite of the forbidden fruit. Her choice opens Eve's eyes to her sin. As a result, she hides herself from God. In the same way the serpent tempts Eve to taste the fruit, Satan tempts us to eat the fruit of comparison.

Satan works so hard to convince us that our self-image is best developed by our comparing ourselves to others on social media, TV, movies, and magazines. Worse, he encourages us to compare ourselves with people who really matter in our lives: our friends, family, and other women at church!

Once we taste the fruit of comparison, we either get an inflated ego, or we get it into our head that we don't measure up. In the latter, we forget that God says we are beautiful in His eyes. We begin to operate from an unrealistic, ever-changing secular standard that conditions us to fixate on our flaws, not the grace Christ offers us. Gals, God has sooooo much more freedom in store for us, if we'll only correct our focus!

Let's do an experiment.

Look at the images of these four ladies and answer the questions that follow.

1. Write the first word that comes to your mind to describe each woman.

   Woman A:

   Woman B:

   Woman C:

   Woman D:

2. What criteria did you use to come up with your word for each woman?

Now, let's try the experiment again.

3. Give each woman one more label, only make sure it's positive, not negative.

   Woman A:

   Woman B:

   Woman C:

   Woman D:

As much as I hate to admit it, I struggle with making quick conclusions about other women. When I believe I am "better" than another woman, it is easy to draw a negative conclusion about her. If I believe another woman is "better" than me, I sometimes find myself downplaying her attributes to promote mine. *Do you do the same?*

For example, when I look at the woman in Photo B, I think, "She has let herself go. I don't want to look like that." But when I look at the woman in Photo D, I think, "She's so fit. Look at those abs! But I bet she works out seven days a week and starves herself. I don't have time for that! And I enjoy eating!"

Can you relate? Please tell me that you can relate!

Ladies, we must stop this madness. May our minds be open to God's Word, so that our self-image is based on how He sees us, not as the world sees us. May our eyes be opened to see where our reflection has been marred by wrong thinking.

May we say "No!" to the comparison trap and graciously reflect Christ in what we say and do. May we be women who build up other women, not mentally or verbally tear them down. May we be women who walk in the quiet, humble strength of the Lord so that we bring Him glory.

Reflect

Think about how you tend to view yourself. Does your self-view change because of circumstance? Do you feel good about yourself only when others make you feel good? Do you only feel good when the mirror makes you feel good?

Exercise

Jot down a few thoughts about yourself in each of the following areas:

Your abilities:

Your appearance:

Your personality:

FULL-LENGTH FAITH

Day 2

"I like a full-length mirror because it shows how my top and bottom go together. It shows the whole of me. A half-mirror does not allow me to make sure my top and bottom go well together."

~Betty

Yesterday we talked about our natural tendency to seek out mirrors to validate ourselves. Typically, we study our reflection in our car's rear-view mirror, or the mirror over our bathroom sink. But when we want an aerial view, so to speak, we courageously peek into a full-length mirror.

When we step in front of a full-length mirror, we see ourselves from head to toe. We take in our clothing and our shoes. We scrutinize the way we've styled our hair, and our accessories we've added. "Do I look good?" we ask ourselves. "Do I look young...hip...cool...hot?" Sometimes we also ask our significant others—which makes them sweat! They know that even if they answer, "Yes!" we won't always believe them! For the truth, we need to seek God's Word. It has plenty to say about how God sees us.

Ladies, when we open our Bibles, we stand in front of God's mirror. As we read and study, the Holy Spirit works in our hearts and minds to lead us (Psalm 119:105), guide us in our decision-making (Isaiah 30:21), and reveal the issues in our lives that God wants to work on (Hebrews 4:13) with us. There is nothing wrong with looking our very best. But way more important is how we "look" on the inside. It should be our goal that when we show up in the world, we radiate Christ.

LADIES, WHEN WE OPEN OUR BIBLES, WE STAND IN FRONT OF GOD'S MIRROR.

Let's turn our focus to Paul, the author of Colossians, who went from systematically persecuting the Church to becoming its chief evangelist. In many of his letters, which make up a good portion of the New Testament, Paul teaches us how to beautifully reflect our Savior.

Read Philippians 3:4-6.

1. List some things you just learned about Paul from this reading.

I think it's reasonable to say that Paul's old self-image was wrapped up in his flesh. He zealously opposed those who followed Christ, until he was confronted by Christ on the road to Damascus (Acts 9:1-20). What is clear is that this experience dramatically changes Paul's view of his place in the world. Almost overnight he goes from *persecuting* Christians to *promoting* Christianity! From signing death warrants of Jesus-followers to singing praises to Jesus! From declaring his own greatness, to declaring the greatness of Christ! From not caring what he looked like, but desperate to have his heart reflect Christ.

2. Read Philippians 3:7-9. Record how Paul describes himself after he becomes a follower of Christ.

Paul is willing to lose everything to gain Christ and proclaim Christ to the Gentiles. He no longer looks to his Judaism checklist to define his self-image, but to the full-length truth of the Word of God. In viewing the Old Testament in a new light, his faith in good works transforms to his faith in Jesus Christ.

The Bible tells us that Paul converts a man named Epaphras to Christ during Paul's three-year mission journey to the city of Ephesus. Epaphras is an important figure in Church history, because he returns home to the city of Colosse to share his faith and establish a church.

Located about 100 miles from Ephesus, Colosse was geographically positioned to be influenced by both the west and the east. Numerous philosophies were already popular in this metropolitan city, so no doubt its large Jewish population was regularly introduced to an influx of new ideas and doctrines. Some of these new ideas were causing big problems inside the Colosse church.

False teachers, you see, had infiltrated, promoting the idea that believers need to gain "special knowledge" to demonstrate a higher spirituality. Their teachings later developed into a philosophy called Gnosticism, which asserts that because matter is evil, Jesus couldn't be God because He was human. Other false teachings in Gnosticism:

- The need for observing Old Testament laws and ceremonies, including circumcision, fasting, and internal and external cleansing.
- The worship of angels as mediators to God.
- The promotion of exclusivity; that only a select few could obtain perfection and special privilege.
- The denial of the deity of Christ.

What I find interesting about Gnosticism is the heavy reliance on an individual's efforts and the denial of Christ. Rather than looking into the full-length mirror of God's Word, Gnostics taught that good works reflect one's true spiritual state. In other words, they were telling the Colosse believers that their salvation required more than the security of Christ. This teaching leads Epaphras to travel to Paul's prison cell in Rome, to seek his counsel on how to respond.

Keep in mind that Paul had yet to personally visit the church in Colosse. But he was committed to ensuring that the message of Christ was accurately reflected in their church.

Can you imagine their conversation? Paul, eager to hear all about the church, and Epaphras, desperate for Paul's wise counsel. I picture Epaphras pouring out his heart amidst tears, and the flame of Paul's zeal being fanned as he learns of the false teachers. Paul knows only too well how easily God's truth gets skewed by man! Scripture does not record their conversation, but we do know that Paul was moved to write a letter to the Colossians. Let's dive into his letter.

Read Colossians Chapter 1:1-8

What a stark contrast between how Paul and the false teachers approach the Colossian believers. Paul establishes his apostleship, greets the Colossians, and immediately affirms their faith in Christ. He then opens the full-length mirror of God's Word to remind them of their true reflection. In verses 3 through 8, he shares how he prays for them.

3. Focus on the word "heard" in these verses.

    a. What had Paul heard?

    b. What had the Colossians heard?

4. In whom is the Colossians faith?

5. Where is our hope to be stored?

Epaphras heard the Gospel from Paul. The Colossians heard the Gospel from Epaphras and responded by placing their faith in Christ. The Gospel has been bearing fruit among the Colossians because they have believed they are right standing with Christ. Paul isn't about to let them forfeit that freedom!

6. Does hearing the Gospel make you think differently about yourself?

The phrase "bearing fruit and growing" is meant to make us think of how a fruit tree matures and bears fruit. The Gospel should produce spiritual fruit in our lives, so that we can spread the Good News of our freedom in Christ!

When we are growing and producing good fruit, our self-image becomes solidly connected to what God says about us. What the world says about us loses its grip! Fruit may represent Eve's downfall, but it definitely signifies our growth!

7. How is your life a reflection of the Gospel?

8. Who is one person in your life that you see consistently reflect Christ? List two or three examples of how they do so. Want to make this person's day? Share with them what you wrote down.

In verses 4 and 5, Paul acknowledges the Colossians' faith in Christ Jesus and their love for each other. Paul calls out their faith, love, and hope, which are critical to Christianity. Faith calls us to look to God, love moves us to look outwardly to others, and hope compels us to look to the future.

We have the hope of a heavenly home because Christ willing gave His life as payment for our sin. Christ's sacrifice made a way for us to benefit from a restored relationship with God. His display of outrageous grace, should overwhelm us and move us to love others. It is from this gratitude that we should strive to beautifully reflect Him.

I want to point out that Paul does not use the word "knowledge" in his letter, as the Colossians were hearing that they needed "special knowledge" for God's acceptance. Imagine feeling the weight of having to do enough, say enough, be enough, or give enough to achieve God's acceptance?

If you are like me, you don't have to imagine, because you have tried earning your way to God, and discovered "doing" became an endless checklist of your trying to measure up!

9. Record what you learn about God's grace in the following Scriptures.

   a. Romans 11:6

b. Ephesians 2:8-9

c. Titus 3:5-7

If God saves us by His grace and not our works, why do we so easily get caught up in the "doing"?

Pray. Check.
Quiet time. Check.
Sunday morning church. Check.
Wednesday night church. Check.
Bible Study. Check.
____________________. Check.

It is easy to feel good about myself with so many checks on my "good Christian" checklist. It is also easy to feel terrible about myself when I fail to check them off. Paul reminds me that I need to check my motives. Am I trying to earn my salvation, or accepting that Christ has already graciously done all the work for me?

Reflect

Where do you tend to rely on your good works to feel good about yourself? Do you use good works to try to look "good enough" to Christ?

FULL-LENGTH FAITH

Day 3

"Self-image is hard. We humans, judge ourselves so harshly when we compare ourselves to others. It's such a slippery slope. I leave the house feeling fabulous, run into someone who seems to have it all, and I don't feel so fabulous anymore. But I bet she struggles, just like me."

~Donelle

Oh, don't you and I compare ourselves to others just like Donelle? Think back to when you were a teenager, and how much you worried about being accepted and popular. If you were like me, you worried excessively about your face, your hair, your clothes, *etc., etc., etc.* If you were anything like me, you were constantly checking your appearance in the bathroom mirror between classes.

Think about a popular crowd in your high school? What are some words you would use to describe those students?

- Ability:

- Appearance:

- Personality:

I desperately wanted to be part of the "in" crowd in my high school. In my small town, this privileged group included pretty cheerleaders and buff athletes who seemed to be the life of the party. Because I established them as my standard of who I should be, I constantly compared my abilities, looks, and personality to theirs.

Did this make me happy? I wish. In reality, it made me miserable. My self-image suffered because comparison is painful when you peg yourself on the low end of the hierarchy.

I worked hard on how I looked, and I worked hard to stand out. My husband, Fred, one of my boyfriends back then, says that I was the epitome of "try hard."

- I tried hard to be popular.
- I tried hard to get the highest grades.
- I tried hard to be liked by all the guys.

If you are willing, check any that were a struggle for you.

Oh girls, that last one! 🤦‍♀ I thought guys would like me if I wore more revealing clothing, if I flirted more, if I wore more makeup, and if I said yes to their sexual advances.

But my "try hard" behaviors only left me more empty. I tried to fill my emptiness with under-age partying, but that only left me emotionally fragile. I can look back and so clearly see that I was trying hard at all the wrong things. As my sons are still in school, I can also see that girls are still thinking these actions will still benefit them.

BUT MY "TRY HARD" BEHAVIORS ONLY LEFT ME MORE EMPTY.

What about you? Can you recall a time in junior or senior high when you questioned whether you were talented enough, beautiful enough, or popular enough to be accepted by the people you most wanted to like you? In your adult life now, can you relate to being a "try hard?" Write your thoughts here:

Isn't it hard to look in the full-length mirror of our lives and not find ourselves lacking in at least one area? Do you, perhaps, feel that your thighs are too thick? Your chest too flat? Your nose too wide?

Answer this: By who or what are you currently basing your standard of beauty?

The Colossians were tempted to fall for the "special knowledge" requirement the false teachers were requiring. To be "in the know," they were being told to become "try hards." Epaphras had taught them the truth of Christ, but here they were being sold a man-made standard that would dilute the power of Christ in their lives! That's why Paul's response was so swift and direct.

Let's read Paul's prayer in Colossians 1:9-14.

1. Who does Paul ask to fill the Colossians with knowledge?

2. Fill in the blanks, using verse 9. "Fill you with the knowledge of _____ _____ through all ________________ wisdom and understanding."

God is the giver of knowledge for the purpose of changing our lives to His will! Our challenge is that we have our own ideas of how to shape our lives. We want to pursue knowledge on our own terms. Knowledge that helps us to look better in the mirror, so that we feel better about ourselves. We scan the diet books for how to lose weight fast. We search YouTube videos for tips on making more money. We query our Facebook friends on the cool places we should be vacationing.

When will we stop trying to manufacture a self-image we think the world wants to see, and instead live the life Christ died to give us?

2 Peter 1:3 reads: His divine power has given us everything we need for life and godliness through our knowledge of Him who called us by his own glory and goodness.

Our world bends over backward to dilute and distort the simple truth of Christ. It promotes the pursuit of self-enlightenment and special "knowledge," which are pure lies. But, oh, the lies come wrapped in such attractive packaging! The reason we pause to consider them, is because the lies speak to our egos. We think we need what we don't, because we haven't yet accepted who we are in Christ.

The false teachers in Colosse pushed the need for "special knowledge," but Paul knew the Colosse believers already had "everything they need" (2 Peter 1:3). Once anyone is saved, they receive all that they need for growth and maturity in every area of life: vocational, marital, financial, and social.

We are divinely empowered through our knowledge of God. This is not an empty pursuit of knowledge, but an exciting and rich realization that there is always more to learn about God and His will for our lives.

As we grow in our spiritual understanding of who God is, we are more likely to "live a life worthy of the Lord and may please Him in every way (Colossians 1:10)." Our life reflects our full-length faith to a world that is watching.

Today we look at two of five phrases in this scripture that mark a pleasing, worthy walk:

The first phrase is "bearing fruit."

In this metaphor, Christ talks about our growth by saying that He is the vine and we are the branches.

3. Read John 15:5-8 and share what you learn about bearing fruit.

A branch that is no longer attached to the vine withers and dies. If Jesus is our vine and we are the branches, we must remain connected to Him for our spiritual nourishment. We learn His commands by spending time in His Word, and with the help of the Holy Spirit, we are then able to obey those commands.

Galatians 5:16 refers to this as walking by the Spirit. As we walk (live) in the Spirit, we bear good fruit. Are we perfect? No. We fail, time and time again. But our hearts yearn to reflect Christ, so we have more fruity moments than not.

4. List the fruit of the Spirit from Galatians 5:22-23. Which one do you most need to ask God to help you demonstrate in your present season of life?

The second phrase is "growing in the knowledge of God."

This indicates constant growth—much like a fruit tree bears fruit as it grows. Our goal isn't just to know about God, but to reflect God and help others to do the same.

Ladies, to grow in our knowledge of God, we must intentionally yield to the Spirit of God and allow God to work in us. As Christian singer Tobymac puts it, we have to give God the wheel—and not try to take it back as backseat drivers.

EACH STEP WE TAKE IN LIVING OUT WHAT WE KNOW ABOUT GOD CULTIVATES OUR BELIEF AND STRENGTHENS OUR FAITH.

Each step we take in living out what we know about God cultivates our belief and strengthens our faith.

I continue to see the blessings that come with intentionally yielding to the Spirit of God. For example, I recently said yes to the Spirit's prompting that I fly east and minister to my cousin. She was battling stage 4 metastatic breast cancer. Within a week, God made a way for me to secure a flight, transportation, and lodging so I could fulfill an item on her "bucket list": meeting me in person. What an opportunity it gave me to grow in the knowledge of God's faithfulness!

Ladies, we need experiential learning opportunities like this! When we choose to take steps of faith, trusting God in every detail, we more clearly reflect how Jesus walked during His earthly life. My cousin died just months later. I'm so thankful I yielded and trusted God.

Reflect

Think on a recent experience in which you intentionally yielded to the Spirit of God. How did it affect your trust in God?

FULL-LENGTH FAITH

Day 4

"Self-image is über important. It impacts how we do everything, every day of our lives. When I slink back to a negative self-image, everything suffers. My relationships, my business, and my personal life all suffer as I fight what feels like depression."

~Juli

Gals! We've talked about some tough stuff so far! About our inherent need to seek validation from the world—and our yearning to be "in the know" of what's popular. That we seek out opinions and validation from the world, forgetting that only God's standard matters. We too often reflect the world's values, not God's. Like Juli said, a correct self-image is "über important," because it determines how we show up in life.

WE TOO OFTEN REFLECT THE WORLD'S VALUES, NOT GOD'S.

Yesterday we looked at the first two phrases of Paul's prayer, and his concern that the Colosse church would lose the truth of Christ. It's still a valid concern for us today, as we hear new teachings, both inside and outside the Church.

Using Colossians 1:10, write the two phrases below:

- Bearing ___________________ in every good work.
- Growing in the ___________________ of God.

Just as full-length mirrors reflect our appearance, Paul's prayer is that our lives would reflect our trust in the knowledge God.

Is this hard for us, or what?! There are so many sources available to us to grow our knowledge. Whether cable news outlets, online news sources, or self-help books, we do not lack for knowledge. The question we need to diligently ask is, "How reliable and tested is that knowledge?"

I recently spent some time studying research by world-famous apologist Josh McDowell, which confirms the authenticity of the Bible.[2] In his 50 years of biblical research, Josh has used three tests to determine the reliability of a historical text, whether biblical or non-biblical.

Let's look at each test, and how the Bible continues to pass them with flying colors.

1. **Bibliographical Test**. This test looks for how many manuscripts exists for a text. Does just one manuscript say something, or are there lots of manuscripts saying the same thing? It turns out that there are more than 24,000 surviving manuscripts of the New Testament! This speaks to the credibility of accuracy of the scribes who copied the manuscripts. These scribes were extremely disciplined in producing an exact copy, but their work was still checked and vetted by other scribes before it was deemed a reliable copy. Scholars are unanimous in agreeing that the accurate copying of these Hebrew texts over so many centuries is a phenomenon unequaled in the history of literature.

2. **External Evidence Test**. This test looks for external documents that confirm a biblical text. There are more than 32 historical, non-Christian authors that reported on events and people highlighted in the Bible. This "outside proof" further adds to the accuracy and reliability of Scripture.

3. **Internal Evidence Test**. This test considers a document reliable until proven unreliable by confirmed inaccuracies. For example, when the Dead Sea Scrolls were discovered in 1947, fragments of every Old Testament book was discovered, except Esther. And the Book of Isaiah was dated at 125 BC. When it was compared to an existing scroll dated at AD 900—a whopping 1100-year gap—it was found to have only one difference: a 3-letter spelling difference for the word "light." That is amazing to me! Over an 1100-year period, the meticulousness of the scribes was maintained.

Gals, the Bible is a trustworthy knowledge source. Just as Paul passionately encouraged the Colossians to grow in the knowledge of God, we should read our Bibles to grow in our own knowledge of God.

Let's read Colossians 1:9-14, to focus on the last three phrases of Paul's prayer.

The first is "being strengthened with all power according to His glorious might."

In the original language of these verses, there are three different words used for "strength." Let's look at each of the meanings in the Blue Letter Bible.[3] It is one of my favorite online resources for studying Greek and Hebrew root words.

"Being strengthened" is *dynamoō*: to make strong, to enable, strengthened
"Power" is *dynamis*: strength power, ability.
"Might" is *kratos*: force, strength, might. (Used only for God in the New Testament.)

1. Turn to Ephesians 1:19. Fill in the blanks below, noting the same root word usage.

   His incomparably great ___________/*dynamis* for us who believe. The power is like the working of His mighty ___________/*kratos*. (NIV)

2. Turn to Ephesians 3:16. Fill in the blanks below to see by whom we receive this power.

   I pray that out of His glorious riches He may strengthen you with power/*dynamis* through His __________ in your inner being. (NIV)

God has all the strength/*kratos* needed to make us strong/*dynamoō*. It is through our belief and willingness to yield that we tap into the Spirit's power and unleash God's "glorious might" in our lives. It is the supernatural power that God used to raise Christ from the dead and return Him to the right hand of God. It is through this power that God reveals Himself to us, and strengthens us to shine for Christ! Ladies remember, we reflect what we think, so let's be women who mirror the beauty of Christ's light.

3. Where in your life do you need to be strengthened by God's supernatural power in order to best reflect Christ?

The next phrase is "That you may have great endurance and patience."

The God-given strength that we just learned about above produces great endurance and patience. What's the difference in these words? Let's look at two important distinctions.

- Endurance (*hypomonē*) points to steadfastness in the midst of our difficult circumstances. When we are unwilling to change from our deliberate purpose and we are loyal to our faith and devotion regardless of our greatest trials and sufferings. This means to "remain under" or persevere while trusting that God is not surprised. God is working His perfect will in our lives through the difficult pressures of life.
- Patience (*makrothymia*) points to long-suffering regarding how others' actions affect us. This literally means "a slowness in avenging wrongs."[4]

4. Share a time when you showed endurance in your circumstances and/or tolerance for someone who was trying your patience.

The final phrase is "joyfully giving thanks to the Father."

We have direct access to our Heavenly Father. The false teachers are teaching the Colossians to go through hoops to get to God. But the truth is that believers have direct access to Him—which should fill us with immense gratitude.

Gratitude for God's presence, His provision, His purpose in every circumstance, and His lavish love, demonstrated for us through Christ. No wonder Paul calls us to "joyfully give thanks."

5. In Colossians 1:12-14, Paul gives four reasons for us to show God thanks. Write them here.

Just as a child born into a royal family is qualified to live in the palace, born again believers in God's family are qualified for an eternal heavenly home. Satan tries to overcome us in this world with sin and moral darkness, but God divinely rescues us from Satan's grip.

As believers in Christ, we are qualified, rescued, transported, redeemed, and forgiven. When I place those powerful truths in the same sentence, I am overwhelmed by God's goodness. God chose each of us "before the creation of the world to be holy and blameless in His sight (Ephesians 1:4)."

It is in this knowledge that we should have the joyful thanks that Paul encourages. And we should never let the world make us forget that we are full of God's goodness and light! Let's reflect it bright!

Reflect

Today ponder the importance of positive self-talk. What influences are you allowing into your life that feed you a negative self-image? The TV shows you watch? The music you listen to? Your friends or family members? Your boss? How often do you find yourself thinking bad thoughts about yourself? Is negative self-talk your default?

Exercise

Let's build your habit of positive self-talk! Stand in front of a full-length mirror and speak aloud the words of encouragement you need to develop and maintain a healthy self-image. You can use the suggestion below to help plan your "pep talk."

- Tell yourself about your positive qualities.
- Focus on two or three strengths that you have, and talk through how you can further develop them.
- Remind yourself that you are fearfully and wonderfully made, and that God has a unique plan for your life.
- Recount successes you've enjoyed, and what God taught you in the process.
- Thank God for each area of your life, and commit to defining personal goals and objectives that are reasonable and measurable that will help you grow into your best self.

FULL-LENGTH FAITH
Day 5

"Relentless, repetitive self-talk is what changes our self-image."

~Denis Waitley

I believe we do need relentless and repetitive positive self-talk to build a healthy self-image. I would add that we need self-talk *based on the truth of God's Word.* Speaking of self-talk, how did you do with your reflection exercise yesterday? Did you find it difficult to talk nicely about yourself? Or did it feel uncomfortable, because it felt like bragging?

Take five minutes at your tables to discuss the self-talk exercise. Jot down your primary take-aways after listening to what is shared.

Let's start today's lesson by reading Colossians 1:15-18.

These four verses represent Paul's main emphasis, which is the exaltation of Christ. Rather than attacking the false teachers who were denying Christ's deity, Paul exalts Jesus and shows His preeminence.

Paul reminds the Colossians of the truth of the Gospel message, and in whom they have faith. It is important to remember that we are not saved by our faith in a set of doctrines. Our commitment is to the historical person of Jesus, our risen Lord.

You and I are guilty of breaking God's Law. Satan seeks to steal, kill, and destroy us, but Christ came to give us abundant life (John 10:10). When we place our faith in Christ, and believe that He has paid our ransom on Calvary, we are set free. Free to shine His light, despite our human failings.

Let's look at the evidence Paul provides to anchor Christ's preeminence. The false teachers don't stand a chance!

1. Look up the word "preeminence" in a dictionary, and record the definition below.

2. Record two facts about Jesus using verse 15.

I remember when I first started working on memorizing these verses. The imagery of Christ being the visible representation of God fascinated me. The assertion that Christ was involved in creation, but that He Himself was not created, intellectually challenged me. The claim that Christ is before all, and the reason all things hold together, inspired me to press in and deepen my understanding of Him.

Jesus Christ is God in human form. The record of His earthly life provides us with an accurate image of God, while also displaying His preeminence in three ways.

Jesus is preeminent in revelation.

God chose to reveal Himself to man through Christ. I like the way The Living Bible states John 1:18: "No one has ever actually seen God, but, of course, His only Son has, for He is the companion of the Father and has told us all about Him."

The false teachers believe that matter was evil, and that it's impossible that God would come to earth as a human. Paul refutes their teachings, by stating that Jesus revealed God to us by being a visible representation of the invisible God.

3. How does Jesus describe this in John 14:9?

Jesus is preeminent in creation.

Jesus is "the firstborn over all creation" (Colossians 1:15). This means that Jesus was uncreated. It is important to understand that the word "firstborn" means Jesus *preceded* all creation, which means that He is *sovereign* over all creation.

The false teachers deny that God created the world, because He would not create evil. So their teaching says that Jesus, as a created creature, is just one of many intermediaries between God and humanity. Paul refutes this by stating, in Colossians 1:17, that Christ is before all things, and in Him. All things hold together. John 1:3 also states this truth plainly: "Through Him all things were made."

4. What things were created by Him and for Him, according to verse 16?

So far we have covered two very important truths. First, that God is revealed through Christ, meaning that Christ is God. Second, that God and Christ created all things. What fascinates me is that we can know God through our study of Christ, and we are part of the "all things" created.

5. How should knowing that you are created by Christ, exist for Christ, and are held together by Christ, impact your daily living? How does this knowledge motivate you to better reflect Christ?

Jesus is preeminent in headship.

Christ is the beginning and head of the Church. The Church is often referred to as "the body of Christ." It is composed of all true believers who trust Christ and receive the Holy Spirit. The false teachers refuse to see Christ as the source of salvation, claiming that one can only find God through "special" knowledge. Paul refutes their teaching by proclaiming that Jesus is our only means of salvation. Jesus is the "firstborn from among the dead" (Colossians 1:18). He died a physical death, but through His resurrection triumphed over death.

6. What did Christ's resurrection accomplish, according to Hebrews 2:14-15?

This passage in Hebrews makes me think of the lyrics of the song "Death Was Arrested" by the Georgia-based contemporary worship band, North Point InsideOut.

We have life because Jesus conquered the grave! Jesus triumphed over death, so that you and I can step out of our prison of poor self-image and reflect the hope we have in Him.

Girlfriends, when people try and trample on our Christ-reflected image, let's be like Paul!

Let's step in front of our full-length mirrors and declare Christ's preeminence in our lives. We are created in His image, *we are who He says that we are*, and our lives will NOT be defined by the chains of comparison. We are forever free in Christ!

FREE IN JESUS

Jesus triumphed over death, so that you and I can step out of our prison of poor self-image and reflect the hope we have in Him.

Reflect

Offer Christ thanks for releasing you from a "prison" in your past. How does your freedom impact how you see yourself now?

"Work on being in love with the person in the mirror who has been through so much but is still standing."
—Author Unknown

BE A MAGNIFIER

Day 1

"Work on being in love with the person in the mirror, who has been through so much but is still standing."

~Author unknown

Self-Image can be tricky. Since it is based on our own view of our abilities, appearance, and personality, what happens when one or more of these aspects change? It makes sense to say that our self-image is likely to change as well. Perhaps the anonymous person quoted above experienced this. Clearly, he or she had withstood many obstacles.

You and I also have been through a lot. Life is always changing, right? People come and go in our lives, sometimes even our best friends, children, or spouses. Sometimes it's a job we lose—or worse, our entire life savings. Even the good health we're enjoying today might turn into a dire diagnosis tomorrow. Every obstacle we encounter has the potential to skew how we see ourselves—unless we ground ourselves on an unshakeable foundation.

EVERY OBSTACLE WE ENCOUNTER HAS THE POTENTIAL TO SKEW HOW WE SEE OURSELVES—UNLESS WE GROUND OURSELVES ON AN UNSHAKEABLE FOUNDATION.

I firmly believe that the Bible is that trusted and unchanging source. Because God is unchanging. He is the same yesterday, today, and tomorrow. No matter what battles you and I are facing, we can trust that He is securely holding us. How does that truth make you feel?

Let's look at Psalm 19, to understand how God's Word is the sure foundation for our self-image.

Using verses 7-14, answer the following questions about God's Word.

1. Name the six titles given the Word of God in verses 7-9. Also note how each title changes us. I've given the first one, as an example.

   a. The law of the Lord is perfect. God's Word revives the soul.

   b.

   c.

   d.

   e.

   f.

Now let's look at each phrase and its importance to our understanding of a self-image based on God's Word.

The first title is "The law of the Lord is perfect, reviving our soul."

Today, "the law" refers to the whole of Scripture, which is free from corruption, filled with all good, and perfectly suited to keep us on the path God has for us.

2. What does 2 Timothy 3:16-17 say about Scripture?

You have likely heard that all Scripture is inspired by God, and is useful in many ways. Daily, we should be willing to allow the Bible to teach us, rebuke us, correct us, and train us in righteousness. When we choose to submit ourselves to the perfect truths of God's Word, we are revived. In the original Hebrew, the word "revive" used in Psalm 19:7 means return, or turn back.

This suggests that the Psalmist knew of our human tendency to get off course. Seriously, gals, have you ever gone for a walk and decided to explore off the well-worn path? Or decided that a shortcut was worth the risk? I sure have! And I have the muddy boots to prove it!

It is a GOOD thing when God course-corrects our lives! What I have learned in my own life is that God's course-corrections strengthen my faith, deepen my trust in His plan, and help me to establish correct boundaries about my abilities. I believe that the more we see God's way as the "perfect way," the more secure our self-image becomes.

The second title given the Word of God is "The statutes of the Lord are trustworthy making wise the simple."

3. What does Psalm 9:10, 31:14, and 56:3 say about trusting God?

The Bible can be trusted because God can be trusted. God breathed each and every word of Scripture for our good and His glory. When we are humble, simple, and open to biblical teaching, we are made wise by His Word.

Self-audit: Do you view the Bible as offering you incredible wisdom for how to handle modern life? Why or why not? Take a moment and discuss this at your table.

The Bible's wisdom can help us in so many ways. It brings us to a saving relationship with Christ. It can guard our hearts and minds as we fight the comparison temptation. It can keep us from thinking more highly of ourselves than we ought. It helps us to see ourselves the way God sees us—each with our unique gifts and skills and talents. All of the personality bits He intentionally birthed us with to accomplish His purposes!

The more we live by God's Word, the more our self-image is shaped by its wisdom. Gals, there is no better place to root our view of our abilities, appearance, and personality than in Scripture. And because Scripture is unchanging, no matter how much change happens around us or in our lives, we can stand firm on its truth and strength. The world constantly changes its definitions of "success" and "beauty," but God does not. What a relief.

THE MORE WE LIVE BY GOD'S WORD, THE MORE OUR SELF-IMAGE IS SHAPED BY ITS WISDOM.

The third title of God's Word is "The precepts of the Lord are right, giving joy to the heart."

4. Record Psalm 119:159-160 below.

Scripture is true and in perfect alignment with God's picture view of the past, present, and future. This allows Scripture to reveal a true image of good and evil throughout all of time, but also to pin-point the good and evil within our own hearts. This is a good thing!

Jeremiah 17:9 characterizes the heart as deceitful above all things and beyond cure, unless we allow God to work on us. Verse 10 says that God searches our hearts and examines our minds to reward us. When we choose to study Scripture with a yielded heart, God is able to reveal our sin issues, refine our character, and shape our personality to best reflect His loving nature.

A personality based on the unchanging Word of God leads to a self-image based on God's strength. A self-image that allows us to look in the mirror and know with certainty who we are, because we know with certainty whose we are. That brings joy to the heart.

The fourth title given for God's Word is "The commands of the Lord are radiant, giving light to the eyes."

5. What does Matthew 6:22-23 say about the eyes?

Jesus is addressing the issue of spiritual vision. The Holy Spirit can give us the capacity to see as God sees, and do as God desires for us to do. The challenge is choosing to push past everything that can cloud our vision—including our agenda, our reputation, our wants and needs, and our aspirations. When we get self-absorbed, we become like a mirror in a bathroom after a hot shower has been taken with the door closed. Rather than clearly reflecting Christ, we project a foggy image to others.

The fifth and sixth titles are "The fear of the Lord is pure, enduring forever" and "The ordinances of the Lord are sure and altogether righteous."

6. According to Psalm 119:9, how do we keep our way pure?

The word "fear" in this verse is one of reverence and awe of God. The word "pure" means to cleanse, to clean up morally or physically. The word "sure" means truth, firmness, and reliability.

God's Word is sure, never changes, and works as a cohesive unit even though it is made up of 66 books written by 40 authors. Its reliability as a document of truth continues to be reinforced by historical evidence discovered and vetted by scholars. We can trust that the Bible is "altogether righteous."

When we keep our lives according to God's Word, we can expect it to cleanse us, empower us, and equip us. This is why we need Scripture so desperately!

Reflect

Which of the six titles of God's Word gives you the most delight in understanding the value of the Bible in your life? How do the titles magnify the importance of the Bible to you?

BE A MAGNIFIER

Day 2

"I do not use a magnifying mirror. They're scary! I'd rather stay in denial. Seeing all those up-close blemishes and wrinkles—yikes!"

~Renae

Magnifying mirrors: women either love them or hate them! In a social media post I asked women to share what they think of magnifying mirrors. Renae bravely shared her response above.

1. What's your reaction to magnifying mirrors? Do you love them or hate them? Write your thoughts below.

Yesterday we established that God's Word is the best foundation for our self-image. And that God's Word serves as a magnifying mirror in our lives. God's Word points out the spiritual blemishes and wrinkles in our thinking. Perhaps this explains why many Christians don't like to spend much time in the Bible. Too many want an easy Christianity, not a daily walk with Christ that includes conviction and teaching.

But when we read, study, and apply God's Word to our lives, God transforms our image to true beauty.

Let's read Colossians 1:19-20.

The false teachers in Colosse are asserting that the spirit is good, but that all matter (including humanity) is evil. So, they assert, Christ could not have been both fully God and fully man, because God is holy and people are not. Paul refutes their argument when he declares that "all fullness" dwelt in Jesus Christ. Let's learn more about what Paul means.

2. Using the following references, note what you learn about Christ's fullness.

    Ephesians 1:22-23

    Ephesians 3:19

    Ephesians 4:13

The word "fullness" comes from the Greek word *plērōma.* It means that which is (has been) filled. When we find this word in the New Testament, it refers to the body of believers—including you and me—and indicates that we are filled with the presence, power, and riches of God and of Christ. God's fullness was not added to Christ, but a part of Christ's essential and permanent being.

As we learned from Colossians 1:15-18, Jesus reveals God, is the Sovereign Creator, and the Head of the Church. The sum total of all the power and attributes of God are in Christ. That makes Colossians 1:19 one of the most powerful declarations of Christ's deity in the New Testament.

3. According to Colossians 1:20, what has God accomplished through Christ?

4. Define "reconcile" using your dictionary.

5. How does Christ accomplish reconciliation?

6. Recall a time when you worked to reconcile with someone. What were the circumstances? How did you achieve reconciliation?

My husband, Fred, is Filipino. His parents immigrated to the United States not long before Fred and his brother were born. I met Fred when we were both in high school. The first seven years of our dating were filled with heartaches and breakups. Yes, we were really young and immature! We spent a lot of time magnifying what was wrong in each other but I was the one doing the breaking up!

As you can imagine, Fred's father finally had enough of me. One summer he told Fred to stop pursuing me, and if necessary he would fly him to the Philippines to find a wife. He even set Fred up with a local Filipino girl! A girl he thought would appreciate Fred, not take him for granted like I was doing.

But one year later, when Fred and I realized we wanted to stay together and eventually get married, I set out to reconcile with his father. Speaking with him about how I had hurt his son didn't work, so I starting looking for opportunities to demonstrate my commitment to Fred. That summer Fred's dad mentioned that he needed help tackling a yard project. I thought, "This is my opportunity!"

Fred and I traveled the two hours to his house and I spent *several days* pulling up the ferns in his flower beds. It was really hard work, but my putting in those back-breaking hours in the scorching Florida sun helped him to begin to see me in a positive light.

Gals, wouldn't it be awesome if hard work enabled us to repair our image so we could, on our own merit, achieve spiritual reconciliation with God?! Alas, it can't. We can never do enough, say enough, be enough, or give enough to achieve reconciliation with God, apart from Jesus. No matter how much volunteering we do at church—or how much we do to impress our in-laws.

WE CAN NEVER DO ENOUGH, SAY ENOUGH, BE ENOUGH, OR GIVE ENOUGH TO ACHIEVE RECONCILIATION WITH GOD, APART FROM JESUS.

Christ is the chosen and sufficient agent in reconciliation; nothing else is needed, and nothing else will suffice. When Christ died on the cross, He met the just demands of the Law by paying the penalty for our sins. Our acceptance of Christ means that we can begin the process of being changed to magnify Christ. 2 Corinthians 5:17 promises us that anyone who is in Christ "is a new creation; the old has gone, the new has come!" Let's look more closely at what follows that passage.

Read 2 Corinthians 5:18-21 to answer the following questions.

7. What does God commit to believers?

8. What name does Paul use to identify believers in verse 20?

9. Describe in your own words the great exchange that occurs in verse 21.

Reflect

Most people think of an exchange occurring when two things of equal value are swapped. Not so with God. He gives us Christ's righteousness for our worthless sinfulness! What prayer of thanksgiving can you offer Him for this amazing gift, and for a life that can be changed to reflect Christ?

BE A MAGNIFIER

Day 3

"As I have aged, I've found that I need a magnifying mirror every day to put on makeup! I have one mounted on my bathroom wall and a compact for traveling. I can't live without it, even with my contacts."

~Cindy

Aging! Ugh! Unfortunately we can't escape it or the changes that it brings. As Cindy notes, changes in eyesight often cause women who once hated magnifying mirrors to embrace them.

Sigh. I'm sure you don't need me to tell you that our eyesight isn't the only body part that changes with age. Our hair color…our skin … even our memory changes as the years add up. I don't know if you're having a hard time with this, but I will admit that these unwanted changes can sometimes negatively affect my self-image.

Some days it's a battle for me to even get dressed and leave the house! And yes, I totally realize what a waste of time it is to unduly worry about the things that sometimes bug me about my appearance.

Here's my challenge for us: what if we focused less on our external appearance and more on our level of wisdom?

Yesterday we closed our day of study with a look at 2 Corinthians 5:18-21, which calls us to be ambassadors of reconciliation. The word ambassador means "to be older, elder," which suggests experience associated with living longer.

Each passing year also bring us new opportunities to learn and grow to become more like Christ. Our goal, as committed Christ followers, should be transformation in our thinking, to have transformation in our living. Only when we do a good job of reflecting Christ, can we do a good job of serving as His ambassadors.

Let's read Colossians 1:21-23.

1. How does verse 21 describe your condition before being reconciled?

2. What do you think the phrase "enemies in your minds" means?

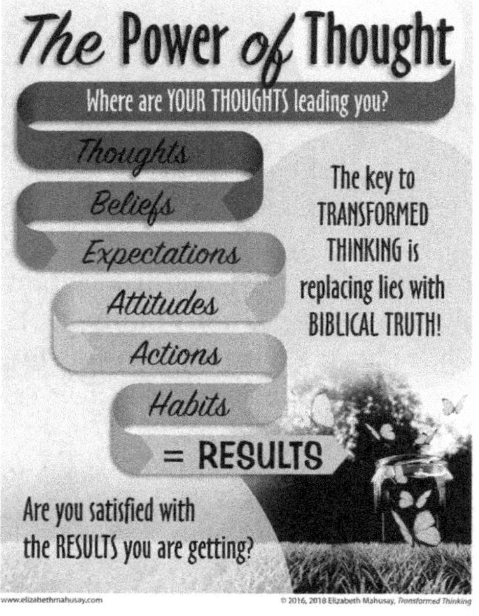

Our very thoughts can make us "enemies in our minds" toward God, as sin corrupts our thinking about God. Take a look at the graphic here that identifies how thoughts lead to actions.

- When we *think* wrongly about God, we *believe* wrongly about God.
- Wrong beliefs lead to our having unmet *expectations*.
- Unmet expectations lead to bad *attitudes* such as disappointment or discouragement.
- Bad attitudes lead to the "evil behavior" referenced in Colossians 1:21.

An endless cycle ensues, unless we allow God to correct both our thoughts and actions.

Think for a moment about a wrong thought you had about God that He graciously corrected. Was it, perhaps, that God wants you to "prosper" above all else? Or that bad things shouldn't happen to "good" people (you)? Briefly discuss this at your table.

Gals, I want you to be clear that "evil behavior" is NOT what alienates us from God. Wrong thinking alienates us from God, which leads to our sinful behavior. This is why I am so passionate about transformation in thinking. We cannot change our poor behavior if we ignore the thinking that led to our actions. Our society continues to ignore this precept and then wonders why it fails!

Let me give you an example of the Power of Thought process I've learned to apply in my life to identify wrong thinking. I start with a negative behavior that goes against God's standard, and drill down to uncover the thought or thoughts that led to it.

Negative Action/Behavior: I don't tithe.
Attitude: I am anxious about our finances.
Expectation: We are going to be further behind.
Belief: We can't afford to pay our bills.
Negative Thought: I question whether God will come through for us.

Now let's take the negative thought and make it positive. We'll work through the steps again to determine an appropriate biblical response, action, and behavior.

Positive Thought: Philippians 4:19 promises that God will supply all my needs, according to His riches in Christ Jesus.
Belief: God is faithful to provide for our needs.
Expectation: When I trust God and tithe, He will take care of me and my family.
Attitude: I have hopeful anticipation that God will work out our finances.
Positive Action/Behavior: I tithe out of obedience to God's Word.

3. Where in your Christian walk do you struggle with living to God's standards? Share your struggle on the Negative Action/Behavior line below. Then use the steps to work backward through the Power of Thought process to identify where your thinking needs to be transformed. You may find it helpful to ask a trusted friend to work through the process with you.

Negative Action/Behavior:
Attitude:
Expectation:
Belief:
Negative Thought:

4. Now take it one step further. Change your negative thought into a positive thought and record it below. Starting with the positive thought, repeat the process.

Positive Thought:
Belief:
Expectation:
Attitude:
Positive Action/Behavior:

You can read a longer overview of the Power of Thought process on my blog post FearFULLy and WonderFULLy Made: https://elizabethmahusay.com/fearfully-wonderfully-made.

YOU CAN READ A LONGER OVERVIEW OF THE POWER OF THOUGHT PROCESS ON MY BLOG POST FEARFULLY AND WONDERFULLY MADE: HTTPS://ELIZABETHMAHUSAY.COM/FEARFULLY-WONDERFULLY-MADE

Did you catch that working through these steps is an *ongoing* process? It takes time, repetition, and accountability, but it's worth your investment. You can use it to experience "no longer being conformed to the pattern of this world, but being transformed by the renewing of your mind" (Romans 12:2).

As you go through the process, identify and reject your wrong thinking. Replace it with the truth of God's Word, and watch transformation occur. The exciting thing: *Transformation in our thinking leads to lasting transformation in our self-image!*

5. Using Colossians 1:22, fill in the three phrases that describe us after reconciliation by Christ.

   a. ______________ in His sight
   b. Without ______________
   c. Free from ______________

God wants us to share in His holiness. Our being holy means that we're set apart, devoted to God. Unfortunately, it does *not* mean that we won't still struggle with sin. But because of Christ's sacrifice, He presents us to God without blemish. God doesn't see our imperfection; He sees Christ's perfection. As a result, there is NO accusation that can be brought against us to keep us from eternally being with God. We are cleared of all guilt! I don't know about you, but at that I joyfully shout, "Hallelujah!"

6. Knowing the truth of verse 22, how will you live your life to reflect that God is working in you?

Before we close out our day, it is important to address the "if you continue in your faith" in verse 23. This phrase does not make our salvation conditional. Rather, "continuing in your faith" means that if we are committed children of God, we will continue in that grounded and settled faith.

I like the New Living Translation: "*But you must continue to believe this truth and stand firmly in it. Don't drift away from the assurance you received when you heard the Good News.*"

Paul is confident that the Colossians will continue in the faith and the reconciliation of the Gospel. His writings should also encourage us to resist the many temptations to "drift away from" what we know about the Good News.

Reflect

When our self-image is based on God's Word, we have a strong foundation for creating a wonderful life. And in knowing that *He says we are enough*—despite our slip ups and sins—we can walk in assurance, not condemnation. Tell God why you're thankful for this assurance!

Exercise

Using the table below, add a check to the left of any statement in which you struggle to see who you are and whose you are. Write out the accompanying verse on an index card and tape it to your bathroom mirror. Say the verse aloud every time you look into the mirror. God's Word is alive. Speaking it aloud will powerfully affect your thoughts and life!

Who Am I	
I am God's Child	John 1:12
I am bought with a price; I belong to God.	1 Corinthians 6:19-20
I am redeemed and forgiven.	Colossians 1:14
I am free forever from condemnation.	Romans 8:1-2
I am confident that God will complete what He started in me.	Philippians 1:6
I am God's workmanship.	Ephesians 2:10
I am born of God; the evil one can't harm me.	1 John 5:18

BE A MAGNIFIER

Day 4

"How wonderful it is that nobody need wait a single moment before starting to improve the world."

~Anne Frank

Anne Frank received a diary on her thirteenth birthday. She wrote to pass the time during the two years that she and her family spent hidden in a dark, damp, secluded portion of the building that had housed her father's business.

After her family was discovered and forced into a Nazi concentration camp, Anne's diary was saved by a family friend. Sadly, Anne wasn't able to reclaim it; she died just days before the concentration camp was liberated. But since its publication, Anne's diary has been translated into 67 languages, allowing her words of love and hope to continue to positively impact the world.

What a great example of someone choosing to magnify goodness during such an evil period! Like Anne, you and I can choose to stay joyful, whatever our circumstances. And when we base our self-image on the assurance we have in Christ, we become magnifiers of Him to the world.

AND WHEN WE BASE OUR SELF-IMAGE ON THE ASSURANCE WE HAVE IN CHRIST, WE BECOME MAGNIFIERS OF HIM TO THE WORLD.

Let's read Colossians 1:24-28.

Paul endures many challenging circumstances as well. He suffers much for the sake of the Gospel. But because Paul says "Yes!" to proclaiming Christ to the Gentiles, his writings still magnify the Gospel today.

In this section of Scripture, Paul reassures the Colossians that it is his joy to suffer for the advancement of the Church. He isn't rejoicing that he's in prison, but that God counts Him worthy to endure the suffering of imprisonment for His name.

1. Read 2 Corinthians 11:23-28. Record all the ways Paul suffers.

In verse 28 we read that Paul feels a daily pressure of concern for all the churches. He is so focused on his appointed mission, that he is willing to endure whatever necessary for the sake of telling the world about Jesus. Ladies, there will be times when you and I also suffer as we present the Gospel. The Bible tells us this. It also tells us that Christ is with us in the midst of our suffering.

2. Jot down a testimony of how you or someone you know has endured suffering for the Gospel.

Paul desires to present to the Gentiles the "Word of God in its fullness." We studied the noun form of "fullness" in Colossians 1:19 on Day 2 of this week. In verse 25, the word "fullness" is the Greek verb plēroō. It means to make full or complete.

Paul wants to proclaim the entire message of God's Good News which, until this moment, has been a mystery. While the Old Testament does record that Gentiles will be saved (Isaiah 49:6), the revealed mystery is that through Jesus, God will bring Gentiles and Jews to the same level.

3. How long has the "mystery" of Colossians 1:26 been hidden? To whom is it revealed?

The false teachers are promoting an exclusive plan, based on special knowledge they assert only a few can actually discover. (Does this sound like Jesus' message? NO!)

They are saying that knowing God is impossible, unless you are one of the few THEY deem "enlightened." But Paul declares the whole message of God is available to all, both Jews and Gentiles. Today we think this is no big deal, but in Paul's day his invitation to the Gentiles is shocking.

4. Read Ephesians 2:11-12 to better understand the separation between Gentiles and Jews. Fill in the table below, indicating all that separated them. Include what is stated and what is implied in the verses.

Gentiles	Jews

5. Using Ephesians 2:13-16, list all the ways Christ destroyed the dividing wall between the two groups.

Do you now understand why Paul's revealing the mystery of "Christ in you, the hope of glory" to the Gentiles is so revolutionary? Both Jews and Gentiles need Christ. Think of the excitement this message must have generated in the Colossian church full of Gentile believers!

Once these non-Jews had been outside the promises of God. But now they are members of His family! Once they were spiritually dead, but they now have life in Christ! They now have the glorious hope of Christ!

No wonder Paul is passionate about proclaiming Christ. He wants everyone to be "perfect in Christ" (Colossians 1:28). Paul wants the Colossians to live out the truth of "Christ in you, the hope of glory." Through Christ, the Colossians have the very power of God's Spirit working within them. Since God's power is needed to become spiritually mature, Paul is willing to expend every bit of his God-given strength to promote that growth.

Just like Paul, God is asking us to Be a Magnifier of the message "Christ in you!"

In sharing this message with others; however, we will likely experience feelings of inadequacy, fear, or lack of time.

I experienced all of these feelings when I felt the nudge of the Lord to apply for the Women's Minister position at my church. My desire to share the message of Christ had been growing, but I still fought the question of adequacy. I found myself asking, "Who am I and do I have what it takes?" I am thankful that mentors and close friends prayed for me, and encouraged me that God would equip me for whatever He asked me to do. It was a four-month process of praying, seeking, and obeying.

As I write this study, I am now serving in that role for Cottonwood Creek Church in Allen, TX. God has shown Himself faithful to equip me, lead me, and allow me countless opportunities to grow. He has supernaturally stretched my time to serve Him through this role, and I am so humbled and grateful.

I encourage you, dear sister-in-Christ, to believe that God desires to powerfully equip you, as well. He just needs you to be willing. He will supply the courage you need.

6. Is there anything God is nudging you to do, but you feel inadequate?

7. How does knowing that you have "all His energy" encourage you to cry, "Yes, Lord!"?

Reflect

If God's fullness dwells in Christ and Christ is in you, then the fullness of God dwells in you! Spend time reflecting on the fact that all His promises are yours! Record a prayer of commitment to obey Him.

Exercise

Fill in the blanks:

Colossians 1:19
For God was pleased to have ________ His fullness dwell in ________.

Colossians 1:27
...the glorious riches of this mystery, which is ________ in ________, the hope of glory.

BE A MAGNIFIER

Day 5

"Magnifying mirrors show the areas of my face that need attention, such as that stray eyebrow, that little beginning pimple, or that little patch of dry skin that needs extra moisturizer. A magnifying mirror allows me to correct those with ease"

~Karla

We started this week looking at how the Bible provides the best foundation for our self-image. The Bible acts as our magnifying mirror because it shows us our spiritual blemishes, and the wrong paths in our thinking. Let's close the week by looking at how our lives can be a magnifying mirror to the world. If we are to live a life that reflects Christ, we must give thought to our role in magnifying Christ to the world. Let's look at two facets: our presence and our speech.

As you answer the questions below, ponder how you are magnifying Christ in your sphere of influence.

Let's first consider three biblical examples of presence:

1. How does Abraham's presence affect the opinions of Abimelech and Phicol in Genesis 21:22?

2. In Genesis 39:3-6, how does Potiphar respond to Joseph's presence in his home? How does Potiphar benefit from Joseph's presence?

3. What does God tell Joshua in Joshua 1:6-9, and how do the people respond to Joshua in 1:16-18?

Now apply this to your life.

4. Think about when you enter a room. How would you describe the impact you intend to have on the atmosphere in the room? Jot down why you answered positively, negatively, or no impact.

5. Write down the name of someone that you have noticed positively impacts the atmosphere of a room they enter. Specifically describe how they do so. Is it their smile, words, or actions, perhaps?

Our presence should magnify the work of God in our lives.

Like Abraham, we should desire that people see God within us in everything we do. Like Joseph, we should use our presence to benefit the people that God calls us to serve. Like Joshua, we should lead based on our reliance and submission to God's Word.

I have considered the question of how my presence impacts others many times. Too often I enter a room wanting people to notice me. I want to be the center of attention. But in the "I have it all together" persona I often project, people sometimes consider me intimidating. (Yes, that's the word they have used.)

My goal should not be on me getting noticed, but that through my words and actions people notice Christ in me. Gals, I am still a work in progress! But I am thankful for God's gentle reminders to keep Him as my focus, rather than myself.

6. Which Old Testament example from above most resonates with you, and why? Where can you use your presence to impact others? What are some actions steps that you can take to ensure that your presence honors and glorifies God?

The second way we can magnify Christ is our speech.

Let's consider King David's example:

7. What does David desire in Psalm 19:14?

8. Record the connection between the heart and the mouth highlighted in Luke 6:45.

In our highly digital society, we must expand our concept of "speech" to include what comes out of our mouth, and what flows from our fingertips. I'm talking about the text messages and emails we send, as well as the social media posts that we make and respond to.

9. Think of a recent example of how someone negatively influenced a conversation. Specifically describe what they said or wrote, and how that made you or others feel.

10. Share an example of someone who consistently elevates a conversation. Be specific in describing how they do so. Are they polite? Encouraging? Gracious in their responses to others?

It would be nice to tell you that I have tamed my tongue, but here, too, I am still a work in progress. I can be really abrupt when I am tired and hungry. And when I feel my time is wasted, my tone probably makes Jesus wince. *Sorry, Lord!* In both circumstances I often find myself asking for forgiveness because I didn't magnify God.

When I write a text message or social media post, I have to consciously slow down and consider what I have written and how the recipient might receive it. It is too easy for me to skip the cordial introductions and get right to the point.

Many times I have gone back and added a warm greeting at the beginning of my message before clicking the send button.

Can you relate? Please tell me that I'm not alone in this!

In both our presence and speech, let's commit to magnifying Christ well to the world. Our doing so requires that we consistently look into the magnifying mirror of God's Word, so that He can address the issues of our hearts. When we choose obedience to His ways, we can reflect Christ well in every conversation.

Reflect

In your life, which area needs more improvement—your presence or your speech? Over the coming week, ponder any thoughts God brings to your mind.

Exercise

Use any feedback God shares with you to jot down action steps that you feel will help you to better magnify Christ in the world.

"I struggle with self-image because I'm influenced by society, listen to negative thoughts, neglect His Word, and my expectations of myself are really high."
—Suzanne

CRYSTAL CLEAR CHRISTIANITY

Day 1

"I struggle with self-image because I'm influenced by society, listen to negative thoughts, neglect His Word, and my expectations of myself are really high."

~Suzanne

On Facebook I posed this question: "I struggle with self-image because…" I appreciate that Suzanne was so authentic in her response. Veronica and Cathy also shared.

Veronica's self-image developed from the message she heard that everyone else is prettier than she is. This script played continually in her mind as she grew up, forging a negative neural pathway in her brain:

> *"I was compared to the other girls in my family," she shared. "I was seen as larger, shorter, and not as pretty. I've always heard people tell me how pretty my mom and the others are. But people rarely complimented my appearance, so I struggled with feeling less than everyone else. I still struggle with comparing myself to other women. I can have some pretty harsh internal comments about myself."*

Cathy shared that when she was little, her mom was always dieting. While Cathy doesn't blame her mother for the entirety of her struggle with positive self-image, she is aware of the foundation her mom's dieting laid in her thinking:

> *"I always thought my mom was the most beautiful woman in the world," she wrote, "but I wish that food had not been such a focus. As an adult, I struggle with my weight. I have a disproportionate focus on food, and I sometimes reward myself with food. When I'm super busy at work and exhausted, I want to have a great meal. The problem is when that great meal isn't healthy."*

Don't miss that both of these gals accepted these negative messages as truth. They each shared with me their need to be in God's Word to win the battle for their thoughts. And it truly is a daily battle, as negative neural pathways aren't changed overnight. In her book, *Battlefield of the Mind*, Christian speaker Joyce Meyer states, "I want to impress on you the absolute necessity of getting your thinking in line with God's Word. You cannot have a positive life and a negative mind."[1]

I couldn't agree more! What's your gut reaction to that statement?

Let's do some work in this area.

1. Write out 2 Corinthians 10:4-6.

2. What kind of weapons do we need to demolish the negative strongholds in our thinking?

3. How are we to treat every thought?

Ladies, strongholds are built on the negative neural pathways in our brains. These negative thought patterns run counter to what God says about us. Like a soldier ordered to take the enemy captive, we must take captive any thoughts that don't align with God's Word! We make each thought obedient to Christ by replacing it with truth from the Bible.

Below are some examples of enemy thoughts and the replacement truth we need to defeat these lies.

Enemy thoughts	Bible-based thoughts
I have to rush.	I need to be still. Psalm 46:10
I should be fearful.	God reassures me. Isaiah 43:2
I feel pushed to ___.	God promises to lead me well. Psalm 23:1-3
I am so confused.	God enlightens me. Ephesians 1:17-18
I am condemned.	I am forgiven. Colossians 2:13
I am stressed out.	God is my refuge. Psalm 46:1-3
I am discouraged.	Hope in God renews my strength to keep going. Isaiah 40:29-31
I am worried.	Prayer changes how I see my circumstances. Philippians 4:6-7

Change begins with an awareness of our foundational thoughts. *But don't we so often try to change our behavior first?* Gals, we must get to the root that causes the problem! Let's look at how mirrors are made to better understand our own Mirror Image development.

Mirrors begin with a piece of clear glass. The glass is placed on a conveyor belt, cleaned with scrubbing brushes and a special cleaning agent, and rinsed with hot, demineralized water. This cleansing is necessary to ensure that the liquified tin and silver that transforms the clear glass into a mirrored surface sticks. *If the glass is dirty, it won't.*

Think of your life as glass that God desires to transform into a reflection of Christ. As with real mirrors, this requires that we go through a cleaning process. Actually, we will go through a lot of cleaning, perhaps daily, until our final day, because of our human nature.

Let's look at Scripture to further cement this mirror metaphor in our minds.

4. What does Romans 3:23 say about us?

We are born with "dirty glass," so to speak. You will recall that Colossians 1:21 says that we fall short of God's perfect standard. If our lives are to reflect Christ, we need to acknowledge that we need His cleansing. We have to willingly submit to the process, even when it hurts. But we can trust God's cleaning, because we know He loves us.

5. Record John 17:17.

The word "sanctify" means to separate, cleanse externally, and purify internally by renewing our soul, free from guilt of sin. How are we cleansed and purified? By God's objective truth. So our minds, which are innately against God, need to be washed by His Word. Only then are our minds ready for the truth that transforms us into a beautiful reflection of Christ.

6. What do we learn from the following verses about reflecting the image of Christ?

    a. Romans 8:29

    b. 2 Corinthians 3:18

    c. Ephesians 4:23-24

d. Colossians 3:10

Once our minds are open to God, the Holy Spirit is able to conform us to reflect God's glory. We are supernaturally able to put off the "old self" and put on the "new self." This new self is what God desires people to see in our reflection of Him.

Read Colossians 2:1-2.

Paul knows the Colossian Christians have received the Holy Spirit, but that false teaching is now threatening to mar their reflection of Christ. Paul admits he is worrying over believers in Colosse and Laodicea. I love how the Message translation of the Bible communicates the intent of Paul's words in verse 1.

> *"I want you to realize that I continue to work as hard as I know how for you, and also for the Christians over at Laodicea. Not many of you have met me face-to-face, but that doesn't make any difference. Know that I'm on your side, right alongside you. You're not in this alone."*

7. List four purposes of Paul's prayer (verse 2).

    a.

    b.

    c.

    d.

The phrase "encouraged in heart" literally means "to be called beside." This is like a best friend who stands beside you, comforts you, and helps you, whether in sorrow, weakness, or confusion. My friend Theresa, who I first met in church choir, has been a faithful "Paul" in my life.

Back then, at just thirty, I was more than a little prideful about my abilities. Theresa's strong leadership and my "know-it-all" attitude caused us to butt heads on more than one occasion. She graciously often allowed me to be "right," even though I was clearly in the wrong! When we were paired together to write leadership materials for the women's ministry, Theresa was, rightly, hesitant to work with me. But she told me that she came to realize that God was at work in me!

Our extensive time spent studying the Bible began to humble me. God began to show me that I had many enemy thoughts rooted in pride. The Holy Spirit convicted me of trying to control my life, rather than submitting to His leading.

Not only did Theresa acknowledge the clear change she saw in me, she purposefully invested time in me to cultivate the transformation God was making in my heart and mind. We spent countless hours in her home talking about Scripture, and how to intentionally reflect God.

NOT ONLY DID THERESA ACKNOWLEDGE THE CLEAR CHANGE SHE SAW IN ME, SHE PURPOSEFULLY INVESTED TIME IN ME TO CULTIVATE THE TRANSFORMATION GOD WAS MAKING IN MY HEART AND MIND. WE SPENT COUNTLESS HOURS IN HER HOME TALKING ABOUT SCRIPTURE, AND HOW TO INTENTIONALLY REFLECT GOD.

Some people say that they don't need to go to church; that they can worship on their own. That's true, but gathering together serves to place us in close community with other believers. God uses other believers to show us where our reflection of Christ needs to be clarified. My relationship with Theresa is such a beautiful example of that truth.

What a blessing that God created the opportunity for our strong-willed personalities to knit together so that I would gain more maturity and better reflect Christ! Theresa has been and continues to be a constant prayer partner, a source of encouragement, and a consistent speaker of truth into my life! I am a better woman because of her investment in my life.

The Holy Spirit comforts and encourages us through Scripture and caring, involved believers. Paul is an excellent example of what a caring, involved believer looks like. You and I need Paul-like figures in our lives to "do" life. Think for a minute about who has been a "Paul" in your life.

8. Describe what made or makes this person such an effective encourager for you.

Reflect

Refer to the chart in today's lesson. Which enemy thought is most challenging to you today? Who can you come alongside to encourage in their Christian walk? How can you serve as a grace-filled "Theresa" to strengthen this person's commitment to live intentionally for God?

CRYSTAL CLEAR CHRISTIANITY

Day 2

"I've been listening a lot to Joyce Meyers. She has me convinced that when we fully 'get' that the only validation we need is God's, we can get past what others think of us."

~Sheri

I like what Sheri shared to my social media post. Just as clear glass moves along a conveyor belt in the process of becoming a reflective mirror, we have to "get past" or move along in our spiritual growth to clearly reflect Christ.

Paul wants the Colossians to grow spiritually and not be led astray by the untrue promises of the false teachers. Ladies, the same is true for us, as well. You and I need the confidence and deep convictions developed *only* through our relationship with Jesus.

Both come from yielding to Christ. Once yielded, the only validation we'll need to seek is God's.

Read Colossians 2:1-5.

1. For review, to whom is Paul writing (verse 1)?

2. Why is Paul praying and believing for the hearts and minds of these Christians (verse 2)?

The fact that Paul so directly addresses the deception plaguing the Colossians speaks to the real issue here. Deception, you see, rarely remains contained. Inevitably, one person's deception affects others. Like a virus, it spreads.

Since Paul mentions Laodicea in verse 1, and later in Colossians 4:16 requests that his letter be read there, we can infer that the false teachings have spread from Colossians. Paul is adamantly warning these believers to be united, fully assured, and confident of their faith in Jesus Christ. To guard their hearts and minds against false teaching.

Today, we are plagued with many deceptions. The media bombards us with lies about who we "should" be to feel okay about ourselves: we need perfectly toned bodies, extended lashes, and airbrushed makeup. It even dictates how our hair and nails should be styled, and the outfits we should wear. With these examples of "perfection," it makes it so stinking hard to be confident!

WE FIND OURSELVES DAILY QUESTIONING, "AM I EVER GOING TO BE ENOUGH?"

We find ourselves daily questioning, "Am I ever going to be enough?"

This is why we need to keep our focus on Jesus! Only He can point us to the standard we should care about. *Jesus helps us to get our heads straight in realizing that who we are on the inside matters so much more than these exterior adornments.*

9. Let's establish some working definitions for knowledge and wisdom. Ladies, grab your dictionary!

    a. Knowledge:

    b. Wisdom:

Knowledge is the gaining of truth, and wisdom is the application of knowledge. Knowledge is careful judgment, wisdom is careful action. Paul reminds believers to have both.

If we want to "know" the mystery of God, we need to know Christ. It is Christ who reveals to us who God is. John 1:18 says, *"No one has ever seen God, but God the One and Only, who is at the Father's side, has made him known."* Christ is the exact representation of God, according to Hebrews 1:3.

If we want to be wise women, we must act on the revealed truth Paul proclaims in Colossians. Christ is in us, and that knowledge empowers us as we yield to His plan, His way, and His timing. It is an experiential knowing, developed as we cease fighting for control of our lives. Our faith grows as we trust Christ, resting in full assurance that we can know Him fully.

But isn't this our daily battle?

We have full access to all the wisdom and knowledge He wants us to learn. In speaking of this wisdom in 1 Corinthians 2, Paul states that *"God has revealed it to us by His Spirit."* When we accept Christ into our life, we are filled with the Holy Spirit. It is the Spirit who searches all things, reveals them to us, and helps us to understand the wisdom and knowledge that God has given us.

10. What is the role of the Holy Spirit, as described in John 16:13-15?

11. How is the man described in 1 Corinthians 2:14 lacking the Holy Spirit?

Let's put this all together. Christ is God. We are in Christ. The Holy Spirit is within each believer, and the key to our understanding God's Word. What a glorious truth! The challenge is our developing daily discipline to explore Scripture and discover its treasures. Can we be real and admit that binge watching a Netflix program can seem way more fun than exploring Scripture? But the reward for our doing really is way better!

12. Why, in Colossians 2:4, does Paul tell the Colossians that Christ holds these treasures?

The word deceive means to "beguile, deceive by false reasoning, to cheat by false reckoning."[2] The false teachers misleading the Colossians are denying the Trinity and the incarnation of Jesus Christ, and teaching that matter is evil. That's Satan for you! He wants to "beguile you, deceive you, and cheat you" of the life that God has for you.

Gals, are we going to let him succeed? I want to hear you loudly shout, "NO!" Right now, whether in your group or alone in the privacy of your home, shout a big, fat, noisy, "NO!" Satan cannot have our peace! He cannot have our joy! He cannot have our confidence! Not if we turn our hearts and minds to Jesus, and rest in His grace and power.

Sheri shared another thought with me that really hit home:

> "When I logically think on God saying that I'm 'alright,' it's easy for me to believe it. But then my emotions show up and I'm like, 'Who am I fooling? God couldn't possibly think I'm cool!' That's when I need to refocus on what God says. In His Word, God repeatedly promises that He loves and accepts us just as we are, even as He works in us to make us more like Him. If I stubbornly continue to fight God's acceptance, then I have to recognize that I am choosing to waste my time, energy, and peace. God is for us! God yearns for us! God digs us! That's TRUTH!"

Her sentiment captures how we allow Satan to waltz in and "steal, kill, and destroy" our lives with his deceptions. Take a moment to ponder where you, like Sheri, have stubbornly chosen to waste your time, energy, and peace of mind to feel acceptable to God. Record your thoughts below.

There have been so many times in my life that I've been stubborn. In the past, my poor choices set me up for deception, and stalled my Christian growth. Let me tell you this story. It's a doozy!

As I shared earlier, my husband, Fred, and I had many periods of breaking up and getting back together during the years we dated. *I really wanted to get married*, but Fred thought we were too young. One summer, when Fred and I weren't together, I met a man 10 years older and started dating him.

Here's the crazy part: on our second date he asked me to marry him—and I said YES! WHAT?! Talk about stubbornly focusing on a goal without thinking of the consequences!

Ladies, like a toddler determined to climb the stairs that her little body isn't ready to handle, I focused on getting married to the exclusion of all else. I knew very little about this guy, but I was ready to say, "I do." I even went to a consignment shop and bought a $300 wedding dress! Egads, I cringe now just thinking about it!

Rather than going to church, reading my Bible, or praying about this HUGE decision, I stubbornly wasted my time, energy, and peace pursuing a mate I barely knew! Figuring out where he stood with God wasn't on my mind, either! Oh, boy, was I asking for trouble. Looking back, I believe Satan was hard at work, intent on cheating me out of the wonderful life I now enjoy with Fred.

I am so thankful for the six-page, single-spaced letter Fred wrote me, imploring me to not ruin my life with that marriage. I am thankful, too, that my parents asked me to reconsider my decision. God spoke through them—and fortunately I listened. Two weeks after the proposal, I ended the relationship. All these years later, Fred and I can laugh over that short engagement, but it stands as a reminder of Satan's attempt to "steal, kill, and destroy" the good life God intended for me.

Let's look a bit more at our enemy and his evil intent for us.

13. What does 1 Peter 5:8 say about Satan?

14. How are we to respond to Satan's attacks, per 1 Peter 5:9?

Peter exhorts us to be "self-controlled and alert." We need to be looking for the "roaring lion" when he shows up. But to resist Satan and stand firm in our faith, we must seek the treasures of wisdom and knowledge available to us in God's Word. We must pray for God's help in applying His knowledge to our lives, so that we make wise choices.

Girls, God is always with us. We can turn to Him for guidance every single moment.

9. Consider your life right now. Is Satan trying to influence you to make unwise decisions? How can you, instead, seek wisdom and knowledge to help you through this challenge?

Reflect

Recall a time in your life when you were deceived into doing something unwise. What did you learn? What Scriptures helped you to find your way back to God?

CRYSTAL CLEAR CHRISTIANITY

Day 3

"Christianity is knowing, beyond a shadow of doubt, that you have been saved from death and destruction by Jesus Christ's death and resurrection. And then we are called to tell the world of this great and precious gift and Good News."

~Gail

I love the clarity of Gail's response to my question, "What does crystal clear Christianity mean to you?" If we are to reflect a crystal clear Christianity, we need to search out, embrace, and seek to understand the knowledge of Christ in the Bible. Then we can apply that knowledge to live godly lives. Ladies, our walk needs to match our talk, in every way.

Let's read Colossians 2:6-8.

Paul encourages the Colossians to continue to develop their relationship with Christ. To not only receive His salvation, but to then actively live to God's standard. The Greek word "receive" in verse 6 is *paralambanō*, which means to take, receive, to acknowledge a person to be what she or he professes.

Let's learn more about what it means to receive Christ.

1. What do the following verses tell you about people who have received Christ?

    a. John 1:12

    b. Acts 10:43

c. Romans 10:13

d. Galatians 3:26

e. 1 Timothy 1:16

2. What is the recurring theme in these verses?

Our salvation is the realization that we are bound for destruction, because we are dead without Christ. The only way we can be revived is to accept Jesus as Lord. We are not accepting a system or philosophy. We are accepting that Jesus is God in human form, that He lived a perfect life, died a criminal's death, was buried in a borrowed tomb, and rose again to ensure our forgiveness of sins and eternal life with Him.

3. Share briefly when and how you received Christ as your Savior. What was it that made you love Jesus and realize you needed Him as Lord in your life?

I remember attending a special service at my church when I was seven. I realized that night that I was missing something. Though young, I had observed my parent's trust in God. I witnessed their reliance on His faithfulness to provide for our needs. I sensed their deep commitment to being in relationship with Him, and that they made worshipping Him a priority in their lives. My dad and step-mom were mirrors clearly reflecting biblical truth.

At that church service I knew I needed and wanted the personal relationship with Jesus that my parents had modeled for me. I have called Jesus "Savior" ever since.

Christianity, as a religion, has deep historical roots authenticated by both Christian and non-Christian sources. Historical evidence—still being discovered by scholars today—continues to verify the trustworthiness of biblical text and prophesy.

Christianity isn't a man-made religion that demands believers have "blind faith." Yes, believing in Christ's death, burial, and resurrection does require faith. But deep down, as we look around at the intricateness of our world, and witness both large and small daily miracles, our souls confirm the truth of Christ.

Yet we must daily be on guard, ready to fight off the deception of our enemy. Christianity can't be passive to have power, it must be lived on the offensive!

4. From Colossians 2:7, what three actions keep us from being deceived?

 a.

 b.

 c.

As we discussed in Day 2, Satan is set on deceiving us. Let's look more closely at the three actions we can take to prepare for his deceptive schemes so that we recognize when he's trying to mess with us.

First, we need to be rooted.

"Rooted" means established deeply and firmly, like a tree. A tree is a living entity with roots that both anchor it and soak up needed nourishment from the soil. As Christians, we need to grow deep roots in the rich, life-giving soil of God's Word.

The more daily time we spend with Christ, through prayer and biblical study, the stronger, thicker, and deeper our roots will grow.

5. How did Jesus describe Himself to the disciples in John 15:5?

Second, we are to build our life on Christ.

When you build a house, you want to build on a strong foundation. Here in Texas, the soil on which the concrete foundation is poured matters. If there is any shift in the soil, cracks will appear in the foundation, which can impact the entire structure. I've had friends with cracked tiles, cracks that run up their walls, windows that break, and plumbing that leaks to name only a few of the resulting issues.

Just as God's Word is the life-giving soil in which we can grow deep roots, it is also the unshifting soil on which we can build our lives.

6. Look up Matthew 7:24-26. What two actions are we to take to build our lives on a strong foundation?

Third, we are to strengthen our faith.

We can study the Bible our entire life. But if we are to establish our faith, we must live out what we learn! This is how we realize Christ is central in our life: by choosing to trust that He is who He says He is, and that He can do what He says He can do, we wholeheartedly seek after Him.

This active choice to trust God is a continual process that leads to our having correct thoughts about God, ourselves, and life. Our right thinking starts by knowing what God says to us in His Word. As we come to know who God is and what pleases Him, we gain wisdom and knowledge that further strengthens our faith.

HERE'S THE THING, LADIES, SATAN HAS A DIFFICULT TIME DECEIVING THE BIBLE-GROUNDED BELIEVER!

Here's the thing, ladies, Satan has a difficult time deceiving the Bible-grounded believer!

7. On this scale, mark where you are right now in your knowledge of the Bible. 10 represents that you're very knowledgeable of the Bible, 1 represents that you haven't spent much time in the Word.

|—1—2—3—4—5—6—7—8—9—10|

Gals, here's my challenge to you: make it your goal to move closer to 10 in this season of your life. Know the facts of Jesus' ministry and resurrection. Memorize Scripture that reminds you who you are, and how much God loves you. Not only does time in God's Word transform our reflection, it protects us from wasting our time and mental peace on the world's deceptions.

Paul cautions us to not be taken captive through hollow and deceptive philosophy. I believe that one of our greatest struggles today is the deception of Postmodernism. Postmodernism, in simple terms, is analyzing life through the rejection of logic, absolute truth, and objective moral values. The Postmodern thinker claims there is no God, and thus, no absolute standard. "Good" and "evil," "male" and "female," even "right" and "wrong," then become entirely subjective.

Thus, a person gets to establish and live by their own moral and ethical code, without judgement because they are simply following their "truth." To not validate or respect another's "truth," we're told, is to be judgmental, intolerant, and condemning. *Even "unchristian" to some critics.*

Satan pushes this lie. Because if there is no absolute truth, then we all get to be the "god" of our life. If we are our own god, we can't be held to a higher moral standard because *we* are the highest standard. Satan has been so clever in launching this campaign—and harnessing social media to spread narcissism around the globe.

But oh, how good it sounds to be able to do whatever we want, without feeling any guilt about it! At least until our self-absorbed choices cause immense pain and suffering in our lives and the lives of others. *Paul admonishes us to not be taken captive by any false teachings that promote self over God, because the result is never good.*

If we are to have a crystal clear Christianity in a world that desperately needs to see Christ, we must gain wisdom and knowledge from the Bible and other trustworthy sources. Ladies, just because we hear a teaching on TV or read it on social media does not mean we should take it as gospel! There are a lot of teachings floating around right now that are being peddled by false prophets. Some may be rooted in Christ, but their human tweaks make them lies. The Church's current attachment to prosperity teachings is one of them.

If we embrace a teaching or an idea that is not entirely of Christ, we end up embracing an empty idol void of genuine spiritual truth, power, and hope.

IF WE EMBRACE A TEACHING OR AN IDEA THAT IS NOT ENTIRELY OF CHRIST, WE END UP EMBRACING AN EMPTY IDOL VOID OF GENUINE SPIRITUAL TRUTH, POWER, AND HOPE.

With objective truth being swept aside, it's no wonder that so many now view the world without hope. If black isn't black, and white isn't white, we end up with an endless choice of grey. Some embrace this, sure, but others discover a painful truth: In creating a life void of absolute truth, they become hyper-aware of their own void—a void never satisfied outside of a relationship with Christ.

Reflect

In our Postmodern world, we must be ready to use our minds, eyes, and God's Word to reflect a crystal clear Christianity. Consider each of the scriptures below and record which one you most need now, and why.

> **Our Mind:** *"We demolish arguments and every pretension that sets itself up against the knowledge of God, and we take captive every thought to make it obedient to Christ."* 2 Corinthians 10:5
>
> **Our Eyes:** *"For our light and momentary troubles are achieving for us an eternal glory that far outweighs them all. So we fix our eyes not on what is seen, but on what is unseen, since what is seen is temporary, but what is unseen is eternal."* 2 Corinthians 4:17-18
>
> **God's Word:** *"Do your best to present yourself to God as one approved, a worker who does not need to be ashamed and who correctly handles the word of truth."* 2 Timothy 2:15

Exercise

Write down steps you are going to take in your area of need to more clearly reflect Christ.

CRYSTAL CLEAR CHRISTIANITY

Day 4

"Here is what I know: There is no vacation, no perfect body, and no amount of success that will fill us up the way Jesus does!"

~Elizabeth

If we want to reflect Christ in our lives, we need to recognize the truth that no thing or person will ever be able to satisfy the God-created ache in our souls. Ladies, that's truth!

Look at the *Chicken Soup for the Soul* book series. A collection of inspirational and motivational stories, *Chicken Soup for the Soul* has over 250 titles, translated into 43 languages, published in more than 100 countries, with more than 500 million copies so far sold around the globe.[4]

Clearly, people are looking to satisfy the ache in their souls.

Let's talk about this ache. It's the deep craving in our soul, the result of the "eternity that God has set in the hearts of men" (Ecclesiastes 3:11). This means that there isn't anything or person in this world that can completely satisfy us. Only God.

But, that hasn't stopped people from trying to find it outside of Him, has it? Our challenge, as believers, is to choose the best nourishment for our souls and to eliminate any source that does not strengthen our relationship with Christ. When we allow someone or something that is in opposition to biblical truth to nourish us, we will have distortions and defects in our mirror image of Christ.

Earlier this week you learned about the process glass goes through to become a mirror. The making of a mirror isn't complete without inspecting it for defects. Any portion of mirror that fails the inspection is cut off. Today, let's consider the importance of cutting out anything in our life that isn't rooted in Christ.

Read Colossians 2:9-12.

Paul is strident in addressing the false teaching on the deity of Christ. Paul knows that the Colossians are hungry for spiritual filling. The challenge with being hungry, however, is we often feel the temptation to feed on worldly teaching. Proverbs 27:7 says, *"He who is full loathes honey, but to the hungry even what is bitter tastes sweet."*

Paul reminds the Colossians—and us, ladies—that the best way to be full is through Christ. *"For in Christ all the fullness of the Deity lives in bodily form"* (verse 9).

1. Turn to Be a Magnifier, Day 2 (page XX), and record the definition of "fullness."

2. Look up each of these verses, and write a truth you learn about the deity of Christ.

    a. Matthew 3:16-17

    b. John 1:1

    c. John 1:14

    d. Romans 9:5

    e. 2 Corinthians 4:4

Jesus is God. He is the sum total of all that God is: all of His being, and all of His attributes. As Paul writes in Colossians 2:10, *"And you have been given fullness in Christ, who is the head over every power and authority."* Ladies, we need to daily ask ourselves if we are allowing Christ's fullness to satisfy our soul ache for wisdom and knowledge.

Let's stop here a minute and talk about the pain we cause by comparison.

When we compare our life with that of others on social media, and conclude that our life is incomplete or lacking, we open ourselves up to the enemy who loves to make us feel that God withholds goodness and blessing from us. He loves to make us feel inferior, dumb, and ugly. He loves to create that itch for wanting more than we have. For living in a spirit of coveting and lack of gratefulness. For living in judgement of God!

Comparison focuses on how we feel rather than on who we are becoming in Christ. Gals, if you haven't learned this by now, lean in close and I'll share an important secret: your feelings often aren't truth.

COMPARISON FOCUSES ON HOW WE FEEL RATHER THAN ON WHO WE ARE BECOMING IN CHRIST. GALS, IF YOU HAVEN'T LEARNED THIS BY NOW, LEAN IN CLOSE AND I'LL SHARE AN IMPORTANT SECRET: YOUR FEELINGS OFTEN AREN'T TRUTH.

I know this full well, because in my current season of life I have found myself sometimes searching for significance by comparing myself to others. Ugh! When am I going to stop that?! Here's what I mean:

> I see other authors with huge followings on social media, enjoying big publishing deals and prestigious speaking gigs, and I think, "I'm an insignificant tadpole swimming in the great big pool of Bible teachers." And while this might be true right now, I KNOW that God has called me to swim in this pool—which is why you have this completed Bible study currently in your hands. This is too much work, for me not to believe it's what God wants me to do!

3. Where are you, right now, comparing yourself to others and concluding that you are incomplete, insecure, or insignificant?

4. How have you dealt with these feelings, especially if you feel God has called you to do what you're doing?

Christ completes us and secures us. Living a life that reflects Christ gives us significance. Let's look at Scriptures that show how Jesus helps us with this.

5. What promise of completion does Jesus make to us in John 15:11? It may be helpful to use the New International Version translation here.

6. What promise of security does Jesus give us in John 10:28-30?

7. What do you learn about your significance from these verses?

   Genesis 1:27:

   Matthew 10: 29-31:

   Galatians 3:26:

Here's the thing: If we are to bring our best self to the world, we have to make sure our mirror is reflecting who God says we are, and not who the world says we need to be.

8. In Colossians 2:11, what does Christ cut away that allows you to more clearly reflect your relationship with God?

9. In what way are we identified with Christ, per Colossians 2:12?

The same power that God used to raise Christ from the dead, He makes available for our sanctification. Sanctification simply means someone or something used for the purpose God intends. God intends for us to be set apart from the world so that we can reflect who He is.

The more we learn about Christ, the more we become like Him. Think about your driver's license. It includes a photo of you and specific details that identify you. If you don't match the details on the ID, you could be labeled an impersonator. Colossians 2:12 provides the identifying details of being a Christian.

As we accept who God says we are, we begin to look more like Christ. Our very life presents photographic evidence to the world of who we are! As we allow Him to live in and through us, we better reflect Christ to the world.

Our challenge is our tendency to rely on our own power to have victory. We can say we have faith in the power of God, but our actions demonstrate a reliance on our own power. In my teen and young adult years I did a great deal of talking about God and His Word, but my life reflected my living in my own power. I struggled to live out my faith. I would commit to do better, but within a couple of weeks I was right back to my bad habits! That is until I began to fully yield to God's inspection of my life.

Two specific moments are burned into my memory. The first happened on a hot Florida summer day, when I was sitting in church making up a Bible study lesson I had missed.

The lesson discussed the Israelites' cycle of sin and their need to believe God to break free of sin and live in victory. I remember feeling uncomfortable as I sensed the Holy Spirit confronting my own disbelief. It was the first time I realized that I had believed God for my salvation, but for very little beyond that.

It was like, "Thanks, God, I'll take it from here." Not only was I guilty of operating in my own strength, but I would arrogantly take credit for my successes. No wonder I saw very little victory over sin.

I left my church in tears. I sat in the parking lot and confessed my sin of unbelief to God. That day was a personal turning point; I committed to believing God for more in my life. *As I began to walk according to His Word, I began to experience victory over sin!*

10. Can you also recall a moment when the Holy Spirit showed you an area in your life that you needed to hand over to God? Share the moment, and how it has impacted your current walk with Christ.

My second pivotal moment took place almost two years later. My husband was consoling me as we sat at our kitchen table. Tears stung my eyes as I struggled to articulate my thoughts. I felt backed into a corner. I had battled laryngitis for months, which made teaching high school classes incredibly difficult.

I felt God asking me to give up teaching Science, as I felt an increasing desire to write, teach, and speak about my passion for God's Word on a larger scale, but I was dragging my feet. How could I give up something I was so good at? Why would God want that?

"Do you think your season of teaching is coming to end?" asked Fred.
"*But who am I*," I cried, "if I'm not teaching?"

Fred's question helped me to uncover the identity crisis that was hindering my future growth. I was believing that God could orchestrate my next steps, but I hadn't faced the reality that I had tied my identity to my skill and gift of teaching Science. That day I realized I needed to believe God and take steps of faith on the path *I felt He wanted me to take*.

Ladies, here's why I have shared this story with you: Just one month later I submitted my resignation. And almost immediately the women's director of my church approached me to write and teach the fall Bible study for the Women's Ministry. God moved fast once I stepped out in trust. Not only was He stretching me to believe Him for more, He was cutting things out of my life so that I was available to say yes to His best!

11. Can you also recall a specific moment when you followed God's prompting, even though it was hard, and the future unknown? How has it changed your life?

God is so faithful! He has good plans for each of us. When we surrender to Him, we choose to anchor our identity in Christ and Christ alone. I firmly believe that when we take even a single step of faith, believing God is there to equip us, empower us, and energize us, our faith will be deepened and we get to see God move in our lives!

Will it always be easy? No. Faith is never easy. But will it always be worth it? YES!

Reflect

Pray Psalm 139:23-24. Ask God to show you any area of your life in which you are relying on your own power or control.

> [23]Search me, O God, and know my heart;
> test me and know my anxious thoughts.
> [24]Point out anything in me that offends you,
> and lead me along the path of everlasting life.

Exercise

Record what comes to mind, and write a prayer of commitment to anchor your identity in Christ.

CRYSTAL CLEAR CHRISTIANITY

Day 5

"I believe we have to guard ourselves from the noise of the world, which will drown out the voice of God."

~Elisa

Gals, isn't it easy to feel like we're drowning in the noise of the world? There are days when I am around so much noise that it's all I can do to stay sane. I need and crave silence.

What struck me about Elisa's quote is the concept of drowning. Yes, the world can drown out the voice of God, but do we realize the drowned state from which Christ saved us? As we move into our last day of study this week, let's consider a life or death scenario.

Picture this:

> You are stranded in the middle of the ocean of sin, no land in sight, and you are floundering, trying to keep your head above water. Hours pass and you feel the gnawing hunger, and the numbing pain of fatigue in your arms and legs. Your chest tightens from fear of not being able to last much longer. There is nothing you can do to save yourself. Nothing. You cry out, "Jesus, help me!" Suddenly, He's there, His strong arms pulling you from the deep, icy water. "Thanks." you breathe, burrowing deeper into His embrace. "I really needed you!"

Now let's consider the same scenario from a different point of view.

> You are stranded in the middle of the ocean of sin, no land in sight, and you are floundering, trying to keep your head above water. Hours pass and you feel the gnawing hunger, and the numbing pain of fatigue in your arms and legs. Your chest tightens from fear of not being able to last much longer. There is nothing you can do to save yourself. Nothing. Jesus swoops in to rescue you, but you expend precious energy pushing Him away. He offers you his hands again, but

this time you dog paddle around in the water to turn your back on him. "I will save myself!" you assert. "I don't need you!" He can only watch, tears streaming down His face, as you finally sink under the surface of the water.

Which scenario sounds better to you?

The truth: All of us are drowning in our sin until we allow Jesus to tenderly rescue us and give us new life. "He reached down from on high and took hold of me; He drew me out of deep waters" (Psalm 18:16).

THE TRUTH: ALL OF US ARE DROWNING IN OUR SIN UNTIL WE ALLOW JESUS TO TENDERLY RESCUE US AND GIVE US NEW LIFE. "HE REACHED DOWN FROM ON HIGH AND TOOK HOLD OF ME; HE DREW ME OUT OF DEEP WATERS" (PSALM 18:16).

With this imagery in mind, open your Bible to Colossians 2:13-15.

1. Using verse 13, describe your helpless state. Record what Christ did for you.

2. Read Ephesians 2:1-5. Write a description of what it means for you to be dead in your sins.

Paul reminds the Colossians that they are dead in their sins. Just as death leads to the decay of the physical body, sin decays the soul. When Christ died, our sin died. When God raised Christ from His physical death, He also raised us from our spiritual death, and forgave ALL of our sin. Jesus not only took our sins to the cross. He took the demands of the law to the cross.

3. In Galatians 3:24-25, what is the purpose of the law?

4. In Galatians 3:13 and Colossians 2:14, what is nailed to the cross?

The law represents God's holy standard. Because of our inability to perfectly live up to this standard, we have a huge sin debt. The original purpose of the law was to bring people to conscious awareness of their debt. If we don't realize we need saving, how can we receive His gracious provision of salvation? When Jesus died on the cross, He not only removed the barrier of sin that separated us from God, He also removed the law.

5. What three things does Colossians 2:15 say Christ accomplished on the cross?

Jesus won a complete victory over the rebellion of the world when he died and resurrected. He removed the weapons that Satan, the media, or even those posting to our social media can inflict pain on us. But we have to know that He has done so. We have to know who we are in Him.

Have you seen photos of an adult elephant kept in place by a harness attached to just a stake in the ground? The elephant learned, as a baby, that he wasn't strong enough to pull out the stake. Though He could easily free himself now, he doesn't try, because he doesn't believe he can!

Is it any wonder that Paul is so passionate about the Colossians adhering to false teaching devoid of Christ? He wants them (and us) to live according to the victory *already* secured by Christ. But defeated is exactly how Satan wants you to live. His plan is to "steal, kill, and destroy" us. Satan wants us defeated by pride, self-sufficiency, inadequacy, and fear.

I know the reality of feeling defeated. I remember sharing with a couple of friends how frustrated I was at constantly being told that I can appear intimidating. One of my friends replied, "People find you so intimidating because you dress well, speak well, and seem to be perfect. They can't relate to that." "Well that is funny," I retorted, "because when I look in the mirror the last thing I see is perfection."

But later, after reflecting on my friend's comment, I realized that I rarely ever share my shortcomings or failures with others. I too often project that I have it all together, even though I don't. I recognize my imperfection when I look in my mirror, but then stuff it deep inside when I walk away.

6. What does James 1:22-25 say about looking in a mirror?

7. Is there any place in your life where you feel Satan is trying to steal, kill, and destroy you?

I have an example of that from my life. I was going to church, and reading and studying my Bible, but ignoring what God was showing me. I was listening but not doing, rationalizing but not repenting, and forgetting rather than following God's way. So I became an easy target for Satan to attempt to steal, kill, and destroy.

My son, Anthony, was just six months old, and my sister-in-law called asking if I would consider watching Rebekah, her newborn, so she could return to work. I don't think I realized the challenge I was undertaking, caring for two babies under the age of one, but I said yes, without hesitation. I didn't bother to pause and ask God if this was what He wanted.

Satan started shooting flaming arrows of accusation at me. "You are a failure," he whispered. "You can't properly care for two babies." I continued to battle these and other negative thoughts. I felt stuck, mostly because Fred and I really needed the money.

After seven months of allowing Satan to make me miserable about my capabilities, I mustered up the courage to ask my sister-in-law to make other arrangements. She was happy to do so, and God opened a door for the perfect daycare to receive her daughter. God used that season to show me the importance of trusting Him over my own efforts.

Gals, when you and I go our own way without praying and seeking God's direction, we become easy targets for Satan. We can't let our guards down for a second! In my case, I should have opened my Bible ASAP, to gain strength from God's promises, rather than allowing Satan to plant fear in my heart.

The plot of our enemy is to keep you from the full life Jesus has for you. That life is meant to be a reflection of Christ to the world, what I call crystal clear Christianity. I asked readers on Facebook to share what crystal clear Christianity means to them. Katie shared this gem:

"Your mirror image should be how God sees you, not how the world sees you, or even how you sometimes see yourself," she wrote. "The world is cruel in its assessment of our image. To make matters worse, we can be harsh towards ourselves and others. I want the mirror of my life to reflect not only whose I am, but also how He made me—in His own image!!!"

YES! As believers, Jesus saves us from our sins with ceaseless forgiveness. He gives us all we need for a vibrant and full life. Our self-image should reflect this reality. Today, let's commit, through our words, countenance, and especially our thoughts, to reflect who we are in Christ.

May others see, by our crystal clear reflection, that Jesus is the answer to the big questions they've been asking.

Reflect

Share a time where God reminded you of who you are in Him, despite what an unkind person said to you. How did He do so? In His Word? Through another person? Via a poem? In nature?

Exercise

Write out your definition of crystal clear Christianity as a way of creating a mission statement for how you will better reflect Christ going forward. What aspects of your Christianity do you want to be sure you're crystal clear in reflecting?

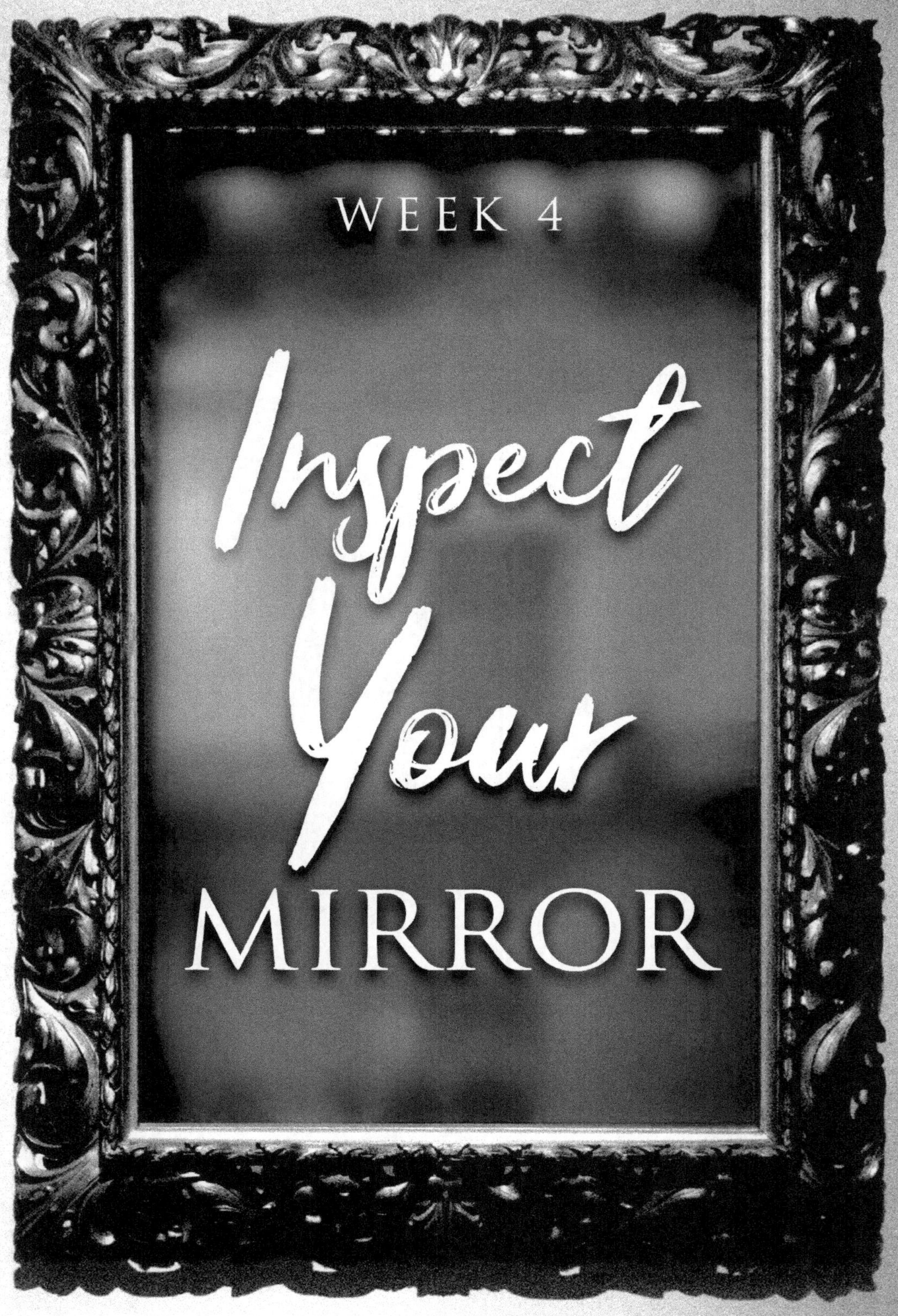

"Every public reflective surface is cause for a quick judgmental glance and critique."
—Donna

INSPECT YOUR MIRROR

Day 1

"Every public reflective surface is cause for a quick, judgmental glance and critique. The mirrors at home always seem kinder. The bathroom mirror is for all levels of facial activities and inspection—the latest fun is chin hair seek-and-find!"

~Donna

Self-inspection. Don't we do it all the time, ladies? There is so much truth to Donna's comment that every "reflective surface" provides yet another opportunity to inspect our appearance. We check the mirror to ensure we don't have spinach in our teeth. We inspect our hair because we don't want it too flat, too big, or too wild. We even glance at our backside, to make sure our skirt isn't caught in our panty hose. Bottom line, we repeatedly inspect our appearance throughout the day.

But do we also inspect our living? After all, it's the things we say and do (or don't say and do) that reflect the condition of our heart and mind. People are inspecting our reflection of Christ to determine if they "buy" the Jesus we claim to represent. Gals, I am sure you are with me when I say that we, as committed Christ-followers, need to cultivate an accurate reflection of Christ to the world.

Like Donna, Abigail responded to my social media post on this topic. I loved that her response was equally authentic:

> *"I'm often taken off guard when I look in the mirror," she shared. "I feel younger, skinnier, and prettier than how I think I look in the mirror. It's this awkward discrepancy—and probably some denial—that keeps me from feeling the unconditional love of God. It also paralyzes me to act in healthy ways."*

Oh, wow! Can you relate? I sure can!

I believe most women experience what Abigail calls "awkward discrepancy." That there is a difference between what we think or feel about our appearance, and what we decide we see in the mirror. Some days, for example, I look at my reflection and think, "Pretty!" Other days I moan, "I am getting old!"

I've coped by changing my makeup products, how I dress, and how I talk to myself. *But what bothers me most is that I can start the day completely satisfied with my reflection, but become quickly dissatisfied if I catch a reflection of myself that doesn't show me at my best.*

How about you? Is your self-view also often conditional on how you think you look?

1. Describe any discrepancies you have seen when you compare your mental view of yourself with the reflection you see in the mirror.

2. How have you coped with "awkward discrepancies?" Have you, perhaps, grown your hair out to hide what you view to be a flaw? Do you wear larger clothing to mask your body shape? Do you try to avoid mirrors, just so your self-confidence doesn't take an immediate nosedive?

Our selfie culture certainly doesn't help us to be less focused on our appearance. You and I could probably take thousands of selfies in our lifetime. And as Donna noted with mirrors, every selfie offers yet another opportunity to critically assess our flaws.

OUR SELFIE CULTURE CERTAINLY DOESN'T HELP US TO BE LESS FOCUSED ON OUR APPEARANCE.

As we've become so obsessed with sharing only the best photos of ourselves, a ton of photo apps have popped up to present us in the best light. Don't like your skin? Smooth it! Think your face is too round? Thin it! Feel the lighting shows way too many crow's feet and laugh lines? Soften or erase them with a filter! In other words, be perfect.

I confess that the "selfie struggle" is real in my own life. It is a running joke with my friend Kelley that when I take selfies of us, I will likely snap 10 or more to get even one photo that we both like!

Ladies, constantly worrying about our looks is exhausting, and our obsession makes us susceptible to getting trapped in the denial and paralysis that Abigail mentioned. What is so powerful about her admission is that when she struggles to "feel the unconditional love of God," her body language reflects her disconnect to the world.

Body language expert Ann Washburn says that our subconscious runs the majority of our body language, and that when we feel weak, we exhibit weak body language. What struck me so profoundly about Washburn's TEDx Talk presentation is what happens when our body language doesn't match our words: People believe our body language over our words.

This validates an expression I often heard growing up: "Actions speak louder than words."

I've observed this truth in my two sons as they have grown up. One of them could be saying what he believed I wanted to hear, but his fidgeting and darting eyes clue me in to question the authenticity of his words. I have been aware of this disconnect in my own self, in the area of sales.

I know, based on my sales training, to speak confidently, clearly, and concisely. I know to ask for the sale. But if I am trying to sell to a person who is able to make me doubt myself, I know that I must fight off the fidgeting and eye darting that will broadcast my doubt or likely lose the sale.

3. Have you ever dismissed someone's words because their body language told a different story? Describe the situation and what the person did.

4. Do you recall a time that your words and body language didn't match up? What caused the disconnect? How did the person you were talking to respond? Describe as many details as you can remember about the situation.

Ladies, our thoughts and feelings affect our interactions, but they also affect our reflection of Christ. It's possible to feel we are an accurate reflection of Christ when, in reality, we are only reflecting ourselves.

For example, we might say, "I can do all things through Christ"—but cower at the first sign of difficulty. Or perhaps say, "I believe God will supply all of my needs according to His riches in Christ Jesus"—but then swipe our credit card instead of waiting on God's supply. Both examples evidence distortions in our Mirror Image.

Though not always fun, inspection of our reflection is a good and necessary thing! We can't change what we don't see—or are unwilling to see. That's why God is always seeking to draw us into a clearer revelation of our sinful nature and need for Him. We need to step in front of the mirror of God's Word and allow God to reveal any discrepancies or denials we hold in our self-image.

Let's declare our willingness to act in obedience to God's commands. Let's ask God to help us break through the fear that so easily paralyzes us, and act with Spirit-empowered determination.

Reflect

I am thankful that I am not where I used to be, and that God's Word continues to lead me to pause and inspect the mirror of my life for distortions. Are you thankful for how God's Word teaches, rebukes, correct, and trains you in righteousness (2 Timothy 3:16)? Is God bringing to mind some areas that you might want to invite Him to help you with?

Exercise

Write out a prayer asking God to transform your awkward discrepancies into beautiful examples of His grace.

INSPECT YOUR MIRROR

Day 2

"No matter how perfect your makeup is or how good you look, that one little thing stuck in your teeth will be the only thing people see when they look at you."

~Karla

I can so relate to Karla's response to my Facebook post about how we use mirrors to validate our self-image. It's hard not to feel judged when our appearance isn't perfect. With this idea in mind, reread Colossians 2:1-12 to refresh your memory on Paul's concern for the Colossians. Then we'll look at how legalism distorts our reflection of Christ.

Paul is determined to address the legalistic judgments prevalent in his day, and the distortions they cause. His heart is to build up the Colossian's faith. The false teachers had likely been relentless in their campaign to draw the Colossian believers back into the legalistic requirements of the law. Paul had taught them that Christ fulfilled what the law foreshadowed, but he now reminds the Colossians that they are free from the law's requirements.

Modern Christians are free from those legalistic requirements. Yet there are still false teachers attempting to draw us into legalistic practices to make us "acceptable" to God. The danger of these false teachings is that they are more about rules than a relationship with Christ.

When we obey rules to the neglect of our relationship with Christ, we miss the bigger picture of the spirit of the law. To better understand that, think about the posted speed limit on a highway.

The speed sign is a statement of what is acceptable when driving conditions are safe. But what happens when there is an accident, or a torrential rain storm? You and I can continue to drive the posted speed limit, but we endanger ourselves and the other drivers around us. In not slowing down, we neglect the spirit of the law, which attempts to ensure the safety of everyone on the road.

Jesus was direct in His rebuke of the Pharisees for their legalism. In Matthew 15:1-9, Jesus calls the Pharisees out for nullifying the word of God for the sake of their traditions. In Mark 7:8, He plainly tells the Pharisees, "You have let go of the commands of God and are holding on to the tradition of men."

Ladies, it is important that we inspect our living for legalism. I don't know about you, but I don't want to nullify the word of God for the sake of a tradition. No wonder Paul is so adamant in reminding the Colossians that Jesus, not these false teachers, offers the truth.

1. Read Colossians 2:13 and record once more what you gain through Christ.

Now read Colossians 2:16-19.

2. Use verse 16 to list all the things Paul admonishes the Colossians to not let others judge about them.

Paul tells the Colossians that these dietary restrictions and appointed feasts are a shadow of the realities to come (Colossians 2:17). A shadow is not a physical object, but an image that represents the form of the object causing the shadow. The object and the shadow are not the same thing, right? Just as there is a difference in the negative of a film photograph and what's captured in that negative.

When Fred and I got married, our photographer captured our special day by using a film camera. After he developed our photos, we received the negatives and a proof book. To relive our beautiful wedding day, I don't pull out the negatives. I pull out the proof book and flip through the printed photos.

The legalistic rituals of the laws in the Old Testament are like negatives. They were ultimately developed in the New Testament when Christ came as God in human form. What the Old Testament foreshadowed, Christ fulfilled. Christ dispelled the shadow; our relationship with Him gives us all we need to know God and please Him.

3. Answer the following questions using Romans 14.
    a. How are we to view others who eat differently? Verses 3-4.
    b. On what basis should we make decisions regarding special days and how we eat? Verses 5-8.
    c. Why are we not to judge our brother or sister regarding these matters? Verses 10-12.

d. What is the kingdom of God, and what is it not? Verse 17.

Isn't it our human nature to be legalistic in our judgments? Yet Romans 14 tells us to make decisions for our behavior based on the reality of Christ, and to trust our brothers and sisters in Christ to do the same. When we do, we more clearly reflect Christ to those who know nothing or very little about Him.

4. What are some things that you typically observe and judge about other women?

I asked some friends via text to share their thoughts on where Christians can be legalistic. Yoana quickly responded with this story:

> *"A friend use to tell me that his denomination doesn't dance and I shouldn't, either. I proceeded to tell him that I wasn't part of his denomination and would end my reply with a dance move! He stopped asking me to stop dancing after getting to know me. It was fun the day we came out of the movies with a group of singles and he dipped me back as though we had been dancing."*

I also grew up under the legalism of "no dancing." I never really understood it because I love music and moving to music. I remember attending high school dances and being one of only a few on the dance floor willing to freely express myself through dance.

Even into my twenties, Fred and I would head to dance clubs to enjoy the music and dance. There are still days at home when he plays upbeat music and I dance in the kitchen while I cook. Of course, my favorite is when he plays one of our favorite slow songs and we snuggle close.

Let's look at some other questions of legalism today. It isn't an exhaustive list, but my desire is to get you thinking about where you may express legalism to your fellow brothers and sisters in Christ.

- Is it ok to drink alcohol or watch an R-rated movie?
- Is one standard of dress more spiritual than another standard?

- Is it ok to listen to secular music?
- Is it ok for Christian parents to spank their kids?

The answer to each one of those questions often has more to do with the weaknesses and strengths of the person trying to answer the question. My weakness in the face of your strength is not a reason for me to impose harsh and legalistic restrictions on you. Likewise, your uncertainty in the face of my certainty doesn't give me license to flaunt my freedom.

Everything that we do should be done to the glory of God. Our reflection of Christ should show our love for one another. As Jesus Himself said, "By this everyone will know that you are my disciples, if you love one another (John 13:35)."

Reflect

Where are you likely to judge someone for a struggle you don't have? Where are you prone to impose rules and restrictions, as if they are commands from God? What is one way you can show love, rather than legalism, to a fellow Christian this week?

INSPECT YOUR MIRROR

Day 3

"I can't go by a reflective window or mirror without glancing over to see myself. If I get into the car, immediately the visor comes down so I can flip the mirror open to again look at what I just looked at a few minutes before in my house. I think it's because I need to be sure no hair is out of place, and no lipstick is on my teeth. Everything about my appearance has to be perfect."

~Carmen

Carmen expresses well the constant pull to inspect our appearance. As we go about our day, isn't our goal to be as perfect as possible? As a society, we sure do chase after it!

Quickly list four things you inspected about your own appearance just this morning:

1.

2.

3.

4.

The important question I have for you today is, "Are you inspecting your mental committee?" What's that, you ask? Your mental committee is basically all the people you allow to influence what you think. Those closest to you influence your thinking the most, but even those you have not personally met have the ability to shape your thinking.

Don't believe me? Let me prove it to you via Facebook.

Let's say I post a hotly debated topic. As my Facebook friend, you react to my post and weigh in by commenting. Inevitably, other people you don't know will weigh in, too. If you choose to read their comments, you will be influenced by the comments that sound logical to you. *Even by people who are posting false information.*

Anyone, anywhere, can apparently now claim to be an expert, even when they're not. Some "experts" sound so educated and logical, that it's easy to buy into their "truth." If we are not careful, we can be deceived by false teachers—or even well-meaning people who don't realize they are helping to spread false info they haven't bothered to vet.

Ladies, it is so important that we are careful where we place our trust.

Let's reread Colossians 2:16-19.

1. In verse 18, how does Paul describe the false teachers?

In verses 18 and 19, Paul provides characteristics of people we should not allow on our mental committee.

The first are persons promoting angel worship.

We can call the false teachers in Colosse promoting the practice of angel worship "mystics." Their teaching is that anyone can have an immediate experience with God or the spiritual world, *completely separate from the Word of God or the Holy Spirit.*

While angel worship isn't common today, worship of nature certainly is. The popular phrase, "Becoming one with nature" is often quoted by those who believe spiritual truth comes from "finding themselves" in nature. These people may pay homage to Mother Earth, but not acknowledge God. Anything we put before our Creator becomes an idol to us.

2. What does Exodus 20:3-4 say about idol worship?

The second are persons with false humility.

The false teachers are offering a self-made religion that serves to magnify themselves, not God. They claim to be humble, but they are incredibly prideful about their alleged visions. They get "puffed up" about their self-importance.

Gals, I'm not gonna lie: I can easily become prideful about what I know or what I believe I can do. Having confidence and being prideful are not the same thing, so please don't think that I'm saying that confidence is bad. God wants us to walk confidently. But when I get puffed up, strutting my ego, I can expect God to "pop my bubble." I regularly remind myself of 1 Peter 5:5: *to clothe myself with humility because God opposes the proud and gives grace to the humble.*

My friend Sheri says that she never fails to trip (literally!) when she gets too cocky. She's so accustomed to being humbled by God this way, that she immediately shapes up!

3. Where might you be tempted to draw attention to yourself rather than to Christ?

Today, you and I need to guard our spiritual lives, being careful in selecting who we listen to, whether on television, social media, or in the books we read. A great question to ask yourself is, "To what or to whom is the person drawing attention?" We could also ask, "Is this person prideful?"

The third are persons who are puffed up.

4. What happens to a person who is puffed up? (Colossians 2:19.)

5. What is the function of the Head/Christ?

False spiritual teachers have no vital connection to Christ. It is all about them and what they can do. We each are limited by our own knowledge, our own strength, and our own weaknesses. We need the empowerment of Christ to live a life that clearly reflects Him. A person who places a greater emphasis on having others follow him or her rather than Christ and His Word should be a red flag to you for potential false teaching.

Living in Texas, I am reminded of David Koresh, once the leader of a spiritual group called the Branch Davidians. David claimed to be a prophet and recruited numerous loyal followers. He also took multiple wives, and was eventually accused of sexual abuse. His false teaching resulted in a standoff with authorities that ended in his death, as well as 79 of his followers.

Another example is Jim Jones. Once a godly pastor, he became a self-absorbed spiritual dictator who committed much sexual sin, among others. Most of his followers lost their lives, at his own order.

Both the Jones and Koresh cases are examples of influence gone bad.

Pause here and consider who is on your mental committee. Consider if they fit Paul's list.

6. Write each person's name below. Are they positively or negatively influencing you? Do they point you toward, or away, from Christ? Should anyone listed be given only limited access?

    a.

    b.

    c.

The reason for our extended consideration of our mental committees is the truth found in Colossians 2:18: "Do not let anyone...disqualify you for the prize." Paul isn't suggesting that the Colossians could lose their heavenly citizenship, but that they could lose the prize of spiritual rewards.

8. Use the following scriptures to list out some things you learn about spiritual rewards.

    a. 1 Corinthians 9:25-27

    b. 1 Thessalonians 2:19

    c. 2 Timothy 4:8

    d. James 1:12

    e. 1 Peter 5:4

Salvation is Christ's gift freely given, which secures our heavenly citizenship. The spiritual rewards we receive in heaven will be determined at the judgment seat of God (2 Corinthians 5:10). Our works will be tested by fire to determine our spiritual crowns (1 Corinthians 3:10-15).

Ladies, we started today listing things we inspect about our appearance. There is nothing wrong with wanting to look great, but let's not neglect inspecting how we live. The works we choose to do, whether good or bad, are directly connected to how we think. Our thinking is directly affected by how well we know the Word of God, and those we allow on our mental committee. False teaching, whether from a church pulpit or our mental committee, can lead to our having wrong thinking. We must choose our influences wisely.

WE MUST CHOOSE OUR INFLUENCES WISELY.

Reflect

Look at your daily life. Where do you try to be perfect? What is your motivation to do so? Is the motivation coming from you, or someone on your mental committee? Do you think the time and mental energy you put toward trying to be perfect is worth it?

INSPECT YOUR MIRROR

Day 4

"In my relationship with my sweet husband, will power was never enough to keep my tongue still. It took God changing my heart and my thoughts toward honor and respect, for my tongue to not only be silenced, but to turn the nag into an encourager and admirer."

~Leslie

Yesterday we focused on inspecting our mental committee to ensure its influence on us is in line with the Word of God. Today, let's inspect our tendency to rely on our own will power. Leslie captures our struggle with will power so well with her quote above.

1. Look up the word "will" in the dictionary and record what you learn.

We can consciously want to change, and make steps to change, only to realize that our will power isn't enough. As we realize this, we tend to double down, work harder, and ramp up our self-discipline and self-denial to try to gain progress. Yet, as Leslie realized, our will power isn't powerful enough.

We need God's power to change our hearts and minds. Ladies, how long will we look to self-help books, magazine articles, or YouTube videos to give us "guidelines" that supposedly bolster our will power? These sources can give us fresh perspective and challenge our thinking, but they will always fall short of changing our hearts and minds, apart from God.

The false teachers in Colosse are presenting their guidelines as necessary for the Colosse believers to grow closer to God. Paul addresses this heresy without hesitation.

Read Colossians 2:20-23 and answer the following questions.

2. List the three "do nots" from verse 21.

3. What are these rules based on, per Verse 22?

4. What does verse 23 way is the worldly appeal of the "do nots"?

Paul is drawing a line in the sand. Just because a teaching comes from a religious source does not mean that it lines up with the whole of Scripture. Asceticism is an example. This doctrine asserts that a believer can reach a higher spiritual state through rigorous self-discipline and self-denial. Thus, an ascetic rejects material comforts as his/her means to develop spiritual maturity.

Christians run the risk of deviating from God's Word when they choose to add requirements of human performance to sanctification.

The standards by which the false teachers are judging the Colossian believers rise from their own skewed teachings. Their teachings of "do not handle, do not taste, do not touch" are void of Christ and assert that works are needed for salvation. Don't we have the same emphasis on earning our salvation today?

Take a look at the "Do Not" list provided here.

DO NOT LIST

DO NOT...

Dance	Drink caffeine	Wear make-up
Drink alcohol	Miss church	Wear pants

5. Are there any "do nots" that you would add to the list?

6. How have you been affected by a church-related "do not?"

I grew up in the church, and my first recollection of a "do not" in our home came from my dad. When I was five, he decided to move to the Florida panhandle to become a commercial fisherman. Going from a guaranteed paycheck to fully self-employed brought a great deal of challenges to our family. *My dad and my step-mom worked six days a week, 12 hours a day harvesting oysters.*

In the shellfish industry, the weather can dramatically affect your income. When it would rain two or three days in a row, the fresh water increase meant bay closures. You can't harvest oysters during that time, which meant my dad earned no income. So on the weekends, my dad also shrimped at night. Getting home after midnight on those days took a severe toll on my parents.

Due to their fatigue, we missed church on a couple of Sundays so that they could sleep in. Then came the explosion. I was sitting in my elementary school classroom, about a mile from the dock where the boat was tied, when it happened.

Dad was working on the boat motor, but he didn't realize that the gas leak had trapped fumes around the motor casing. When a spark ignited the fumes, the motor exploded. My dad was slammed against the boat cabin, which injured his back. My family recognized the unspoken reality that he could have died.

In dad's mind, not only was the explosion a wake-up call from God, but he was convinced that his willingness to miss church was partly to blame. He declared, "We will never miss church!" And from that day on we didn't. No matter how tired they were, we were in church every Sunday.

As a result, I grew up thinking, "Do not miss church. Ever!" *So I noticed when others were not in church.* As I grew older, I began judging my Christian brothers and sisters when they didn't attend. All these years later, I still fight the tendency to judge people when I see they are not in church regularly. This is especially true in my ministry role. I can easily start thinking that ladies who attend church regularly deserve more of my time than those that do not! Even when I don't know what's going on in their lives that might be causing them to miss church. I have no right to judge them.

All a man's ways seem right to him, but the Lord weighs the heart (Proverbs 21:2).

We can create all kinds of "do not" lists and then legalistically watch to see when others violate them. Our judgement may appear wise, but we should ask ourselves why we are playing the role of judge.

7. List at least one "do not" that you have used to judge others.

8. Where did this "do not" first develop? Did you create it, or did you learn it from observation?

9. What is your motive for using this "do not" to judge others? What does it accomplish?

10. Is your "do not" clearly stated in scripture?

The answer to number 10 is really important. Any "do not" that we live by or apply to others that is not based on the Word of God lacks the power of the Holy Spirit to live by it.

This is an important truth when we consider that we live in a culture that is all about self-indulgence. We assert, "I should be able to eat what I want, when I want, regardless of how it affects my body. I should be able to drink what I want, whenever I want, regardless of how it impacts my ability to function. I should be able to have sex with whomever I want, in the way I want, regardless of how it affects me or my partner physically, emotionally, and spiritually."

What is even more troubling is that our "do not" list will never be enough to restrain our "sensual indulgence" mentioned in Colossians 2:23: *"Although these have a reputation of wisdom by promoting ascetic practices, humility, and severe treatment of the body, they are not of any value in curbing self-indulgence."*

As Christians, it is a struggle to battle the rising tide of relative truth, self-expression, and "tolerance." Here's the thing: our will power isn't the answer! The more we rely on our ownselves, the more powerfully sin grips us. Just as Leslie wisely stated, we need the power of God to change our heart and provide the cure for our sinful, self-indulgent nature.

I do want to point out that Paul is *not* saying that rules are bad. In Romans 7:12 he states, "the law is holy." The law helps us to recognize sin, convicts us of sin, provides us with the opportunity to ask God for forgiveness, and reminds us of our desperate need for Christ. But we must be careful in thinking that following the law will save us. Rules cannot save us. Only through Christ do we have salvation.

The power of God within us equips us to curb our sinful appetites and experience victory over sin!

Reflect

Where in your life are you relying on your own will power?

Write a prayer committing to rely on the power of Christ to gain victory over sin.

INSPECT YOUR MIRROR
Day 5

Finally, brothers and sisters, whatever is true, whatever is noble, whatever is right, whatever is pure, whatever is lovely, whatever is admirable—if anything is excellent or praiseworthy—think about such things.

~Apostle Paul

As we close out this week of study, let's review. We each need to inspect the mirror of our life for distortions. We need to often ask ourselves these three questions:

- Are there any distortions of the message of Christ in my reflection?
- Who am I allowing on my mental committee?
- How am I relying on my own will power to gain victory over the flesh?

Today, let's add another layer by asking how our thinking is currently affecting our reflection.

If you recall from the Power of Thought graphic on page 38, our thoughts are the starting point of our beliefs. Our beliefs determine our expectations, and our expectations create our attitudes. Our attitudes lead to our actions. Philippians 4:8, quoted above, reveals that Paul cares greatly about how Christ-followers think.

Read Colossians 3:1-4.

1. What does verse 1 say is the Christian's position with Christ?

2. What do verses 2 and 3 say about where are believers are to set their heart and mind?

As we are raised with Christ and called to set our hearts and minds on Him, let's add context to Paul's instruction.

3. List a truth about Christ you learn from the following verses.

   a. Psalm 110:1

   b. Romans 8:34

   c. Ephesians 4:10

   d. Philippians 2:9

   e. Hebrews 1:3

   f. Hebrews 8:1-2

   g. Hebrews 12:2

   h. 1 Peter 3:22

From these verses we learn that Christ is at the right hand of God in heaven. Christ is our high priest, intercessor, and the author and perfecter of our faith. These truths should become an anchor in our thinking.

Let's look at three thought anchors that are difference makers in our reflecting Christ well.

The first anchor is to think about your position.

Paul says that we are raised with Christ. If Christ is at the right hand of the Father, then so are we because Christ is in us. Paul goes on to say that we should set our hearts on things above. The phrase "set your heart" means to seek so we will find. It is an activity that shows our excitement to seek the spiritual things above.

I make a concentrated effort to envision Christ seated at the right of God. I try to envision what Scripture tells me Christ is doing on my behalf. He is working through the Spirit to cultivate my character and empower my obedience (Romans 8:9-11). He is continually interceding on my behalf (Hebrews 7:25). He is advocating for me when I sin (1 John 2:11-2). Sisters, He is doing the same for you!

4. How does knowing that you are identified with Christ in heaven motivate you to want to seek Him more?

The second anchor is to think about heaven more.

The phrase "set your mind on things above" indicates a setting of one's mind purposefully on heaven. For me, that means spending time thinking about who in my family has gone to heaven before me, and what will it be like to see them again. I think about people I will see there because I shared the Gospel with them. I also spend a lot of time wondering what it will be like to see God in all of His fullness, to praise Him continually, and to experience time untarnished by sin. I can't wait!

Being "heavenly focused" is caring more about the eternal than the temporal. Heaven is our ultimate home, and our lives should reflect our growing understanding that the reality of "there and then" should dictate what we do in our "here and now."

5. How does Colossians 3:3-4 describe your life?

6. How does Galatians 2:20 describe your life?

7. Spend some time thinking about heaven. Record who and what comes to your mind.

The third anchor is to think about your future with Christ.

The day will come when Christ returns. In Matthew 24:30-31, Jesus shares how "they will see the Son of Man coming on the clouds of the sky, with power and great glory." He will gather all the nations, and separate true believers from pretend believers and unbelievers.

Our future includes a place prepared for us by Christ (John 14:3), an inheritance secured by the Holy Spirit (Ephesians 1:13-14), and the promise that He will transform our bodies to be like His glorious body (Philippians 3:21).

I get so excited when I dwell on this future with Christ. I relish the thought of leaving behind the cares of this world to forever worship God! I yearn for the day when there are no more tears, no more sorrow, and no more sickness, because Christ wipes them away (Revelation 21:4). As we think on this glorious future, we are encouraged and empowered to face whatever challenges our current day brings.

Have you heard the expression "You are what you think?" I believe it is true.

When we anchor our thoughts on our position in Christ, on our home in heaven, and on our eternal future with Christ, our reflection of Christ is so much clearer to the world. Ladies, in the same way we inspect our appearance, let's commit to inspecting our reflection of Christ.

Let's humbly stand before the mirror of God's Word and allow it to inspect our lives. Let's look for distortions, for negative influences on our mental committee, and where we rely on will power rather than God's power. Finally, let's inspect our thinking to ensure that we are setting our minds on things above as we walk in obedience here on earth.

Reflect

Review the three thought anchors we covered today. Which one are you committing to think on more?

Exercise

Use the following verses as a mirror. Look into the mirror of each verse, and mark where you are on the spectrum of reflecting what God desires. Record action steps you are willing to take to reflect Christ more fully.

Your Love

1 Corinthians 13:4-7
Love according to the world |——————————| Love based on God's standard

Your Walk

Galatians 5:16, 22-23
Gratifying desires of sinful nature |——————————| Living by the Spirit

Your Talk

Ephesians 4:29
Unwholesome talk |——————————| Helpful talk that builds others up

Your Attitude

1 Thessalonians 5:16-18
Negative about everything |———————————| Joyful, prayerful, thankful

I encourage you to write these scriptures on index cards along with the actions steps you commit to take. Keep your cards close at hand so you can dwell on God's truth.

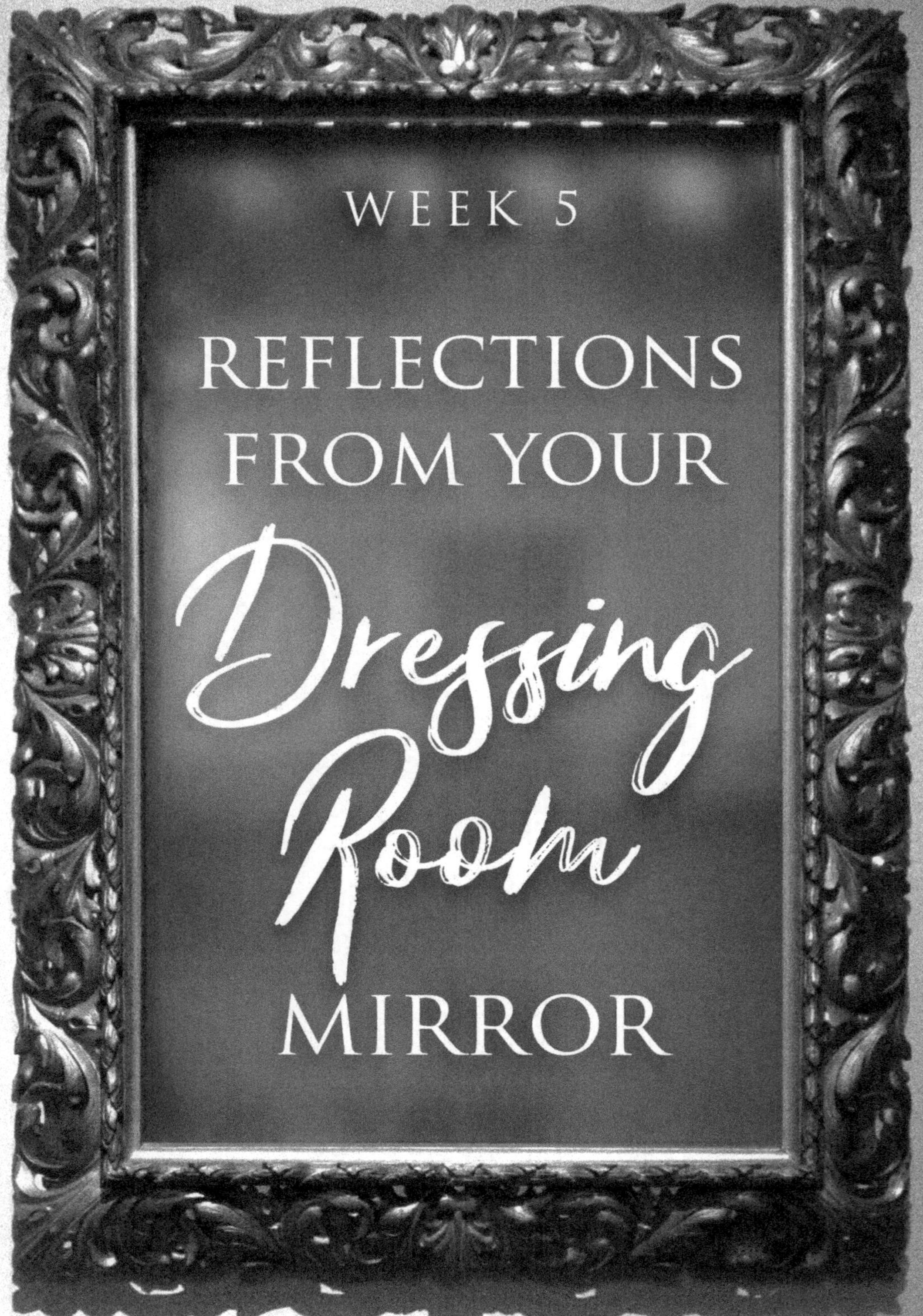

"My daughters checked themselves in the privacy of their dressing room before they made the decision to step out to a public mirror."
—Karla

REFLECTIONS FROM YOUR DRESSING ROOM MIRROR

Day 1

"My daughters checked their appearance in the privacy of their dressing room before they made the decision to step out to the public mirror. Some dresses were a 'no' and not given a chance for others to see. When they were secure with the look, but not sold on it, they stepped out."

~Karla

I was chatting with my friend, Karla, who has raised three girls. She always took her girls dress shopping three times a year for school events requiring formal wear. I asked her how the girls felt about using the three-panel dressing room mirrors found in many stores. She responded with the quote above.

I can so relate when it comes to trying on clothes and deciding what I am willing to walk out and show. My husband wants to see everything I try on when he shops with me, but more often than not, I only allow him to see the outfits I think look good! *Can you relate?*

Table Discussion: Why do you think so many women dread inspecting themselves in dressing room mirrors? What is it about trying on clothes that stresses us out so much?

TABLE DISCUSSION: WHY DO YOU THINK SO MANY WOMEN DREAD INSPECTING THEMSELVES IN DRESSING ROOM MIRRORS? WHAT IS IT ABOUT TRYING ON CLOTHES THAT STRESSES US OUT SO MUCH?

I am betting you have some really good discussion! Let's now move into today's study. This week, as we continue to explore our theme of living a life that reflects Christ, let's keep dressing room mirrors in mind. The mirrors are there to allow us to "see ourselves," right?

The dressing room mirrors are good visuals for how the Bible mirrors to us who God is. The left mirror panel could be labeled the Old Testament. The right panel could be labeled the New Testament. The center panel is Jesus, who is woven throughout the tapestry of the Old Testament and on full display in the New Testament.

God unashamedly presents His truth to us. He desires that we receive it, but He doesn't force us to receive it. Just like so much of what we take into those department store dressing rooms are a "no" for us, we may think we can skip over parts of the Bible because we decide they don't apply to us.

Answer these questions:

1. Are you afraid to trust God because of stories of destruction in the Old Testament?

2. Do you not share your faith because you fear offending others?

3. Do you hesitate to share your Christian beliefs because they differ from the world's?

Let's look at each of these questions.

Are you afraid to trust God?

There are many accounts in the Bible that can leave us feeling uncertain that we can trust God to take care of us. One story that stands out to me is God commanding the Israelites to destroy, by sword, every living thing in Jericho—*except Rahab the prostitute and her household*—because she helped the Israelite spies escape unharmed (Joshua 6:17-25).

Why would God command that even babies be killed? Why would animals need to be destroyed? Can God be trusted to be good to me, my husband, and my children? If I can't understand why all that destruction was warranted, how can I ensure that I don't find myself with the same fate?

Or what about Esther, a Jew, forcefully taken to King Xerxes' palace to be considered for the royal position of Queen. One day Esther is minding her own business, and the next day she finds herself part of the king's massive haram.

Out of all the other young, beautiful virgins also taken to the palace, Esther is miraculously selected by Xerxes to be his queen. But she soon finds herself forced to decide if she's willing to sacrifice her own life to try to halt a plot to decimate the Jewish population with Xerxes' kingdom.

Esther is successful, and God uses her influence with Xerxes to have him proclaim that all Jews have the right to defend themselves—even killing their enemies' wives and children.

Are you, like me, asking, *"How is this right God? Can I trust your judgment?"*

This is the challenge with our uncertainty. What we don't understand in the Bible can cause us to question God's character. As a young and immature Christian, I found myself avoiding reading or discussing topics that made me question God's goodness.

What about you? Do you rope off the parts of God and Christianity that you don't understand so that they don't weaken your faith? Do you think this is how God wants us to address our fears and uncertainties about His love and goodness? Is there a particular Bible story that has caused you to doubt God? Discuss this at your table for a few minutes.

As I started studying and digging into hard passages, I realized that I was in the habit of drawing conclusions *based on my limited knowledge. What I should have been doing was drawing conclusions from the context of the scripture.* Too often we try to interpret the Bible using a modern context, rather than learning about what was happening at the time the text was written.

It is helpful to apply three areas of context when trying to more fully understand Scripture. These are historical context, literary context, and the theological context. Let's reread the passage in Joshua using the proper context, so that we can better grasp the call to destroy the people of the land.

Read Joshua 6:21.

Historical context gives us insight into the historical events mentioned in Bible. Three historical events related to Joshua and the destruction of Jericho:

- God gave the people already living in the land *hundreds of years* to turn from their wickedness (Genesis 15:16).
- At their unwillingness to repent, God commands their complete destruction (Deuteronomy 7:1-6), just as he did when He flooded the earth (Genesis 7:23).
- God warned the Israelites that if these wicked inhabitants were not killed, they would entice the Israelites away from serving Him (Deuteronomy 7:4).

Literary context identifies the genres of literature in the Bible. For example, we find poetry in the Psalms, wise sayings in Proverbs, and historical narratives in books like Joshua. When we understand the genre, we gain insight. Another aspect of literary context is looking at the verses before and after the passage we are reading. Three literary observations about the destruction of Jericho:

- The Canaanites knew about God's ways, but chose not to change (Joshua 2:8-14).
- The Canaanites practiced perverse sexual acts with male and female prostitutes as well as with animals (Leviticus 18:20-24).
- The sins of the Canaanites were a stench to God (Leviticus 18:25-30).

Theological context addresses how the God of the Old Testament is the same God of the New Testament. We best understand the New Testament as we gain understanding of the Old Testament. Think of theological context as themes that can be found in multiple places in the Bible. Three theological themes regarding the destruction of Jericho:

- God is patient and merciful, but He is also just (Genesis 18:25).
- God does what is right. Our limited judgment makes it impossible for us to comprehend His ways (Isiah 55:8-9).
- God judges sin because He is holy (Deuteronomy 7:10; 9:3-5).

The single verse in Joshua 6:21 is best understood when we look at the history of the nations that God told Joshua and the Israelites to destroy. This direct command was the direct result of their unrepentant wickedness. And it shows God's consistency in the expression of His character.

Context matters, ladies. I have found that with each Bible study I take (or lead), I have gained a better understanding of the context behind its stories. I can only expect perfected understanding when I meet Jesus face to face. But until then, I continue to study and seek God's answers for any uncertainty I have.

CONTEXT MATTERS, LADIES.

I remind myself that I can trust that God's ways are higher than my ways, and His thoughts are higher than my thoughts. You can trust Him as well, sisters. Get into God's Word, and study your areas of uncertainty. Don't just skip over troubling passages because they are difficult to understand. Press in and pray for God to open your heart and mind to the certainty of His truth.

Do you not share your faith because you fear offending others?

Most of us are uncomfortable with offending others. And many parts of the Bible are offensive to those who disagree with them. The Gospel itself offends those who don't believe there is only one way to heaven. Yet Jesus clearly makes this assertion in John 14:6: "I am the way, the truth, and the life. No one gets to the Father but through me."

There are many religions that teach many other paths to heaven or paradise. And some religions do not believe in an eternal resting place, good or bad. The likelihood of offending someone is high based on these two points alone.

Before we move on, let's note that there's a difference in biblical truth being viewed as offensive—and our communicating biblical truth in an offensive manner. Reread this truth until it sinks in.

One of the biggest hurdles I had to overcome early in my Christian walk was my offensive delivery of biblical truth. I can look back and clearly label myself as self-righteous. I delivered the truth—but without regard to the person I was trying to evangelize. I was too direct, and often unkind. I was so bent on being right and proving my point, that I didn't take the time to listen to that person's point of view. Ladies, I was not a great reflection of Christ.

What I have learned over the years in my study of Scripture is that our best opportunity to reflect Christ is to follow His example of delivering God's truth. Let's consider when Jesus encountered the Samaritan woman at the well, as recorded in the book of John.

4. Read John 4:4-26 and note as many details as you can about how Christ treated the Samaritan. Keep in mind that as Samaritans were a mixed race, Jews refused to associate with them.

Here's what I noted:

- Jesus went against cultural norms to accomplish the will of His Father. As a Jew, Jesus violated the cultural standard of avoiding Samaritans.
- Jesus engaged the woman in conversation by asking questions. *When we ask questions, we have the opportunity to learn another's perspective.*
- Jesus got her attention by noting her physical need, to highlight her spiritual need. She needed water from the well; Jesus pointed to her need for eternal life.
- Jesus was respectful when confronting her sin: that she'd had five failed marriages and was currently living with a man who wasn't her husband.
- Jesus remained focused, even as she tried to change the topic.
- How Jesus treated her prompted her to take her own counter-culture action.

Do you hesitate to share your Christian beliefs because they differ from the world's?

The Samaritan woman had gone to the well alone, during the hottest part of the day, because she was an outcast in her town. But after her encounter with Jesus, it was to her neighbors that she hurried to share her experience. It was very counter-cultural for a woman in her day to speak to men about doctrinal matters.

But she shared her testimony, saying, "Come, see a man who told me everything I ever did. Could this be the Christ?" The result is that many of the people in her town believed her and hurried to meet Jesus. Think about how persuasive she must have been for them to even listen to her—and to then take action!

5. Look up John 4:39-42. Record the results of the woman's testimony.

Jesus was willing to directly address the uncomfortable topic of sin with this woman. Because she was changed by the experience, she didn't allow what others might think of her to stop her from sharing what happened.

There are many other powerful examples in Scripture of people boldly witnessing on behalf of Jesus. The blind man Jesus healed was ridiculed by the religious leaders, yet it didn't stop him from declaring the miracle Jesus had done in his life (John 9:25-34). Mary Magdalene was the first to see Jesus' after His resurrection, and she ran to share the good news with His disciples. "I have seen the Lord," she cried (John 20:18). And governor Festus accused Paul of being crazy when he shared his testimony of conversion. But his opinion didn't stall Paul's witness (Acts 26:24).

Jesus prepared the disciples for the consequences that their personal witness for Him would bring.

6. Look up Matthew 10:19-20 and record how Jesus encouraged these, His closet companions.

The disciples were arrested, questioned, and persecuted. But they focused on honoring God, not on worrying how they would be received. Ladies, this should be our goal, as well!

Reflect

Where are you likely to struggle with uncomfortable conversations about Jesus, God, or the Bible?

Exercise

Share an example of where you "stepped out" and shared what God is doing in your life, despite how others might react.

REFLECTIONS FROM YOUR DRESSING ROOM MIRROR

Day 2

"As a face is reflected in water, so the heart reflects the real person."

Proverbs 27:19 (New Living Translation)

Yesterday I asked you to reflect on how uncomfortable it can be to initiate conversations about God, Jesus, and the Bible. I'd like nothing more than to sit down with you over coffee or tea to chat about yesterday's reflections!

My prayer is that like the woman at the well, your own encounters with Christ transform you into His image so that you best reflect Him to a world desperate for the hope He unconditionally offers.

Ladies, it's time to have a serious wardrobe assessment. Today I want you to step in front of the dressing room mirror of God's Word and consider what He may be calling you to clean out of your wardrobe.

Read Colossians 3:5-8.

1. What instruction does Paul give in verse 5? How might you explain his command in your own words?

Paul's language suggests a decisive action: the setting of our minds on things above. This sounds easy, but I'm here to testify that it's a moment-by-moment struggle. Paul was forthright in acknowledging his own struggle. Let's read his words in Romans 7:14-25.

2. Let's make sure we have a clear understanding of five sins that should NOT be part of our walk with Christ. Use Colossians 3:5 to write the letter next to the characteristics of the earthly nature.

___ Sexual Immorality	a. Base evil desires that result from poor thinking.
___ Impurity	b. Anything for which there is uncontrolled passion.
___ Lust	c. Disregard for the rights of others in the pursuit of always wanting more.
___ Evil Desires	d. Dirty mindedness, indecency, impurity of thought and speech.
___ Greed	e. Illicit sex between unmarried partners which could refer to adultery.

These five sins run rampant in our modern culture. Watch any mainstream television show, for example, and you will see sex between two unmarried partners, cursing, selfishness, greed, and evil desires being glorified. Real life imitates the junk on the screen. Pornography has become a world-wide epidemic, even inside the Church.

3. Are any of the five sins an issue in your own life? Record why this sin is a stumbling block for you.

You and I inherited a flawed earthly nature. But God sent His Son to provide a way for us to fight the corruption of this world. When we choose to say no to the world's standards, and yes to our freedom through Christ, we gain power, as well as grace from God's judgment.

Ladies, God cannot overlook sin. He is compelled to judge it. Paul's reminder to the Colossians applies to us today: *"You used to walk in these ways, but now you must rid yourselves of all such things as these"* (Colossians 3:7-8).

Paul calls for a wardrobe change. The word rid can be translated "put off, cast off, lay aside," like we do with a grimy, stained garment. We don't try and wash it, we trash it! You moms of boys know exactly what I mean!

4. Let's get even more specific. Use verses 8 and 9 to list and define the behaviors we are to avoid like the plague.

   a.

   b.

   c.

   d.

   e.

What I find intriguing about this list is the progression from thought to action. Let me explain. Anger is uncontrolled temper. It is inward. But as we stew on our anger, it takes root and builds to rage. Rage produces an outburst of action—malice, slander, or filthy language.

- Slander or blasphemy: Speaking ill of others.
- Filthy language: obscene speech, shameful speaking.
- Lying: telling a deliberate untruth, creating a wrong impression by revealing a partial truth, or distorting the facts through exaggeration.

Did you notice that all three actions are connected to our mouth? Yikes! Our mouth too often gets us into serious trouble, ladies!

5. Look up the following verses and record what you learn about your mouth.

    a. Proverbs 21:23

    b. Ephesians 4:25

    c. Ephesians 4:29

    d. Colossians 4:6

    e. James 3:10

We must stand in front of the dressing room mirror of God's Word and honestly assess what we need to cast off! Let me humbly admit to you where my mouth can really get me into trouble: not being transparent.

I am really good at listening to other people's problems, you see. I enjoy solving problems and helping people move from where they are to where they want to be. But my challenge, if I am not walking in the Spirit, is to avoid transparency about my own issues. I'd rather not acknowledge my problems or sins to anyone! Because if I don't, I can perpetuate the impression that I have it all together… which I assure you, is just smoke and mirrors, baby! I have mastered the ability to keep my flaws hidden as much as possible. I've learned to exaggerate my successes, to make myself look (and feel) better. But my not being real clothes me in filthy garments that I must be intentional in casting off.

Reflect

Imagine you are studying yourself in God's dressing room mirror. Think back to a recent conversation. Were your words positive or negative? Did they build up or tear down? Do you sense God nudging you to cast off any filthy garments caused by your mouth? Is there anyone perhaps, that you need to seek out to ask for forgiveness for something you said?

REFLECTIONS FROM YOUR DRESSING ROOM MIRROR

Day 3

"When I think of three-paneled dressing room mirrors,
I think of trying on wedding dresses.
Of finding the perfect one that I would wear to marry the love of my life.
I remember feeling like a princess in a fairytale."

~Erica

I, too, remember feeling like a princess as I stood in front of the dressing room mirror in my wedding dress. That moment made me so excited for my wedding day. When it finally came, I did not put my wedding dress on over filthy clothes and walk the aisle with unwashed hair. No! I took great efforts to ensure that my hair, make-up, and accessories magnified the beauty of my wedding gown. I wanted Fred to see that I cared enough to prepare for our special day. As the doors of the chapel opened, I wanted him to gasp in wonder! I still love looking through our wedding album to relive our wonderful day.

Ladies, the care we give to looking great on our wedding day is the same care we should give to looking great before our Holy God.

Yesterday we looked at how our mouths can mar our reflection of Christ. Today, let's assess whether we're dressing in a way that honors God. If we are to reflect Christ well, we need to exchange our filthy rags to beautifully reflect Christ.

Read Colossians 3:9-11.

1. What exchange is described in verses 9 and 10?

These verses provide an important example for the need for an exchange or substitution. Paul calls us to take off the old self and substitute/replace it with the new self. Think of it as a wardrobe change. We need a willingness to stand in front of our mirror and assess our wardrobe, to remove any items counter to God's Word, so that we can replace them with items of truth.

Those listening to Paul's message would have been familiar with the practice of animal sacrifice, as required by Jewish law. Before Christ, animal sacrifice was God's provision for restoring relationship. A person's sin was transferred to the animal and sacrificed so a right relationship could be restored with God. This process was repeated over and over to atone for sin.

But God was after much more than the ritual of sacrifice. He desired the condition of each person's heart to be right before Him. We see this in 1 Samuel 15:22, which states, *"Does the Lord delight in burnt offerings and sacrifices as much as in obeying the voice of the Lord? To obey is better than sacrifice, and to heed is better than the fat of rams."*

The sacrificial system was always meant to show the inward faith of the individual seeking God. But when Jesus came as God in human form, He forever satisfied the need for animal sacrifices. Hebrews 10:10 states, *"And by that will, we have been made holy through the sacrifice of the body of Jesus Christ once for all."*

God's judgement of our wickedness is death, but Jesus satisfied our debt through His death on the cross and His resurrection from the grave. Our faith in Christ paid God's holy and just demand, allowing us to benefit from the glorious exchange. In taking our sin, Jesus dresses us in His righteousness (2 Corinthians 5:21).

Let's explore the idea of exchange further.

1. Read the following verses and list a truth you gain from each about exchanging the old self with the new self.

    a. Romans 6:6-7

    b. Romans 7:4-6

    c. Romans 8:5-8

    d. Romans 12:1-2

    e. 2 Corinthians 4:16

    f. Galatians 2:20

    g. Galatians 5:24-25

    h. Ephesians 4:22-23

The truths you just listed make it clear why Paul so often wrote about our need for Christ. It is only through our faith in Christ, and the empowerment of the Holy Spirit, that we can successfully "get rid" of the old self and "put on" the new self.

And just as we need to replace dirty clothes with fresh clothes, our new self must continually be renewed, if we are to walk in obedience to God's commands. In other words, you and I must be intentional in closely walking with Christ. Daily we must set our minds on Him, and His ways.

2. What are some ways you intentionally set your mind on Christ each day?

3. Are there areas in your life where you struggle to relinquish control to the Holy Spirit?

4. Can you share a victory you have experienced with putting off your old self to put on your new self? Have you broken a bad habit, perhaps, or successfully added a good one?

There are two significant daily practices I've implemented to set my mind on Christ and release control to the Holy Spirit.

The first is starting my morning with devotion and prayer. As I brush my teeth every morning, I read a daily devotional by Oswald Chambers titled *My Utmost for His Highest*. This gets my mind focused on biblical truth, so that I can then focus on prayer in my prayer closet. I journal a prayer response to the devotional, and spend time praying for those on my prayer calendar.

Starting my mornings this way has made me more aware of my sin, and my need to confess sin more specifically. I recall a pastor once remarking that "many Christians like to "wholesale" confess their sin, when what they need is a healthy dose of "retail" confession. "Father, please forgive my sins" is not specific, and makes it way too easy for us to minimize our sin. Retail confession requires that we be specific and own up to our violation of God's standard.

My heart is to confess as quickly as I feel the conviction of the Spirit. This keeps short accounts and doesn't leave room for Satan to accuse me. For example, recently I was frustrated with a work situation. I felt I was being required to jump through unnecessary hoops to accomplish what was needed for my project. I found myself complaining to some of my coworkers about the situation on more than one occasion.

A few days later my morning devotion centered on Philippians 2:14-15, which says, "Do everything without complaining or arguing, so that you may become blameless and pure, children of God without fault in a crooked and depraved generation, in which you shine like stars in the universe." Ladies, as soon as I read this Scripture, I felt convicted!

Let me take you through my mental steps of how I "get rid" of the old self and "put on" the new self.

A. I confess my sin of grumbling and complaining, and agree with God that my thinking was a dirty garment.

B. I repent by humbly handing that dirty garment to Christ. I envision myself taking it off and laying it at the feet of Jesus.

C. I visualize Christ destroying that soiled garment and handing me a spotless, new garment from the truth of His Word.

D. I take steps to restore the relationship with anyone I may have hurt with my sin.

The steps included my writing a note to the person with whom I was frustrated. I sought forgiveness for my grumbling and complaining. I also acknowledged my wrong attitude to other coworkers to whom I had complained. Girls, I went from being so tied up in knots, to feeling unfettered freedom and joy! When we take steps to quickly address our sin and make things right, God is pleased.

The second practice that has been a difference maker in my life is substitutionary thinking. As I consider my thoughts, I ask God to help me identify which thoughts are true and which are lies. I reject the lies and replace them with truth from God's Word.

Here are some of my favorite substitutionary verses that I use to set my mind on things above. I have personalized them for greater impact in my thinking, so they won't exactly match any Bible translation you might be using.

Lie	Scriptural Truth
I would never do or say such and such.	**1 Corinthian 10:12-13** Lest I think I am standing firm, I am not! No temptation has overtaken me except that which is common to man. But God is faithful; He will not let me (Elizabeth) be tempted beyond what I can bear. But when I am tempted, He will also provide a way out so that I can stand up under it.
I would never survive a loss like that, a diagnosis like that, etc.	**2 Corinthian 12:9-10** God tells me that His grace is sufficient for me, His power is made perfect in my weakness. Therefore, I will boast all the more gladly in this difficulty, so that Christ's power may rest on me…for when I am weak, then I am strong.
I don't have the time, resources, energy, money, etc. to participate in that.	**2 Corinthians 9:6-11** Elizabeth, if you sow sparingly you will reap sparingly. If you sow generously you will reap generously…God is able to make all grace abound to me, so that in all things at all times, having all that I need, I will abound in every good work. I will be made rich in every way so that I can be generous on every occasion, and the recipients of my generosity will result in thanksgiving to God.
My needs are important.	**Philippians 4:12-13** God has seen me through needy times and times of plenty. The secret to contentment, regardless of my situation, whether well fed or hungry, whether living in plenty or in want, is that I can do all things through Christ who strengthens me.
My contributions should be recognized.	**Colossians 3:23-24** Whatever you do, Elizabeth, work at it with all your heart, as working for the Lord, not for men since you know that you will receive an inheritance from the Lord as a reward. It is the Lord Christ you are serving.

5. What Scripture have you used to renew your mind and develop your new self?

What I love about God's Word is that it is for everyone. Every person reading these words has been uniquely created by God. Our experiences are different. How we think is different. Each of our needs are different. But God's Word universally applies to all of us!

He's not a "one size fits all" kind of God. He intentionally creates us with unique personality quirks, body shapes, and giftedness. But He wants us to seek a common goal: better reflecting Christ.

6. List the differences Paul addresses in Colossians 3:11. What is common to all believers?

Oh, that we would see this truth lived out in our culture today. There is so much division in the world. People want to put us in boxes: "*What is your spiritual practice? What is your political party? What is your stance on abortion, gay rights, and animal rights?" They decide, from our answers, whether to accept or reject us. But don't we, too often, do the same?*

As believers, what if we chose to be renewed in the knowledge that "Christ is all, and is in all?" *What if we didn't allow our differences to be barriers of how we treat others?*

AS BELIEVERS, WHAT IF WE CHOSE TO BE RENEWED IN THE KNOWLEDGE THAT "CHRIST IS ALL, AND IS IN ALL?" WHAT IF WE DIDN'T ALLOW OUR DIFFERENCES TO BE BARRIERS OF HOW WE TREAT OTHERS?

Ladies, Christ is the catalyst who brings each of us together, unifying us through Himself. Christ slays the sins of our old life. Christ throws away the garments of our sinful attitudes and actions, after we willingly hand them to Him. Christ renews our minds, thus empowering us to clearly reflect Him. Our collective reflections of Christ brightly shine light in a dark world.

Reflect

Where do you tend to place emphasis on another person's differences? How does it affect the way you treat them?

Have you seen it become a barrier to your reflecting Christ?

Exercise

I dive deeper into the substitutionary process in my book, *Transform My Thinking, God.* Check out the "Intentionality Mindset" lesson on the "Bible Study" page of my website (elizabethmahusay.com). The mindset works!

REFLECTIONS FROM YOUR DRESSING ROOM MIRROR

Day 4

"Our lives are like photographic plates, and prayer is like a time exposure to God. As we expose ourselves to God for a half hour, an hour, perhaps two hours a day, His image is imprinted more upon us. More and more we absorb the image of His character, His love, His wisdom, and His way of dealing with life and people."

~Kent Hughes, senior pastor emeritus, College Church

I love how this quote expresses the profound impact that our spending time with God has on our reflection to the world! The more we absorb of Him, the more our living clearly reflects Him to a desperate world.

When I step in front of a dressing room mirror, I want it to give me a clear picture of my appearance. But I'm often caught off guard by how permitting others to see the clothes I'm trying on makes me hyperaware of what I don't like about each outfit. *Can you relate?*

Spending time with God also makes us hyperaware. Here's what I mean: Here I am, going about my life—making decisions, having conversations—but then I find myself convicted as I spend time in God's presence.

Ladies, the mirror of His Word can make us painfully aware of our ill-fitted clothing of poor choices, careless words, and wrong thoughts. Oh, how we need a continual wardrobe change! We need to strip off the unholy garments that mirror the world, and put on God's custom-made garments that reflect Christ in our lives.

Today, let's study these custom-made garments and how they equip us to do life God's way.

Read Colossians 3:12-14

Let's start with the first word of verse 12: "therefore."

When you see "therefore" in Scripture, it points to the passage that appears before it. A look back provides context for what follows. Take time to read Colossians 3:5-11 as reference. When Paul wrote "therefore," he was referring to all that he had written about discarding the old self to put on the new self.

1. What does verse 11 say are the labels that Paul tells the Colossians church to set aside? After you list them, add some labels that are prevalent in our world today.

Paul reminds the Colossians that *"Christ is all, and is in all."* In effect, Paul is saying, "Put on the clothes Christ has made for you, because they will bring you peace."

2. Write out the three foundational garments that are highlighted in verse 12.

Therefore, as God's __________ people, __________ and dearly __________.

We are a chosen people. Jesus expresses this in John 15:16, as He teaches His disciples: *"You did not choose me, but I chose you and appoint you to go and bear fruit—fruit that will last."* We are meant to be a holy people. We are often referred to as "saints" in Scripture. Paul asserts that God sees us as holy in Ephesian 1:4: *"For He chose us in Him before the creation of the world to be holy and blameless in His sight."*

And God loves us dearly. John 3:16 tells us, *"For God so loved the world that He gave His one and only Son, that whoever believes in Him shall not perish but have eternal life."* Romans 5:5 adds, *"God has poured out His love into our hearts by the Holy Spirit, whom He has given us."*

Knowing that you and I are chosen, holy, and dearly loved should build our confidence! Confident in who God is and who He made each of us to be. Confident in His faithfulness, His provision, and our equipping.

Were you ever chosen to be on a team? I remember being on a kickball team in elementary school. We all just got together and decided it was a good use of our recess. There was no formal "try out," just a willingness to follow the rules, kick the ball, and help your team win.

In middle school I tried playing volleyball and basketball, but I realized that I lacked natural ability. And I wasn't motivated to improve. But when I got to high school, I tried out for the band and was selected. I absolutely loved it! Every time I put on that marching uniform I felt a sense of pride. I wanted to practice to improve my skill because I represented the "Blazing Blue" band!

3. Describe how being chosen for a task or team in your past made you feel. Were there specific expectations you tried to live up to when you were in uniform?

Christian sister, YOU are on God's team!

He chose you.

He clothes you with a custom uniform with His image imprinted on it.

He loves you so much that He orchestrates your life so that you can share Christ with the world that so desperately wants to feel loved and accepted.

In my high school band, the director called the shots. In today's professional sports world, the team owner holds ultimate authority. As Christ-followers, God is the owner of our "team." He has the final say. As teammates we wear identical uniforms, though we each have our specific position. Our uniform sets us apart from all other "teams," as should our behavior. Christ should be on full display if our goal is to reflect Him well.

Let's look at each part of our Christian "uniform," and how it guides us in reflecting God's standard.

4. Use verses 12-14 to list the holy garments Paul directs us to wear.

Reflect Christ in how you treat others.

The first two pieces of our uniform are compassion and kindness. Compassion means "tender mercy." Today we might hear someone say, "This breaks my heart," as they express how deeply they have been affected.

Kindness is "moral goodness and integrity," which leads to unselfish thoughtfulness toward others. Wearing Christ's uniform should compel us to think of others more than ourselves. Philippians 2:4 notes, *"Each of you should look not only to your own interests, but also to the interest of others."*

Reflect Christ in how highly you view yourself.

The next two pieces are humility and gentleness. Humility is "an outward expression of an inner attitude of placing one's self last." Being humble doesn't mean we think poorly of ourselves, but that we have "an accurate estimation" of ourselves. Peter reminds us to do this.

5. Read 1 Peter 5:5-6 and record why Peter encourages us to have humility.

Gentleness or meekness, is power under control, which allows us to consider the needs of others. It is the opposite of arrogance. Paul trained Timothy to seek meekness (1 Timothy 6:11), and to instruct others in doing so (2 Timothy 2:25).

Reflect Christ when you are treated unkindly.

The next three pieces of our uniform are patience, bearing with one another, and forgiveness. The Greek word used here for patience is *makrothumia,* and it relates to having patience with people. Inevitably others will provoke you and make you angry. Makrothumia speaks to how to correctly respond to this provocation: God wants us to respond with self-restraint, not go on the attack. Paul prayed for the Colossians to have this patience.

6. When we're provoked, what does Colossians 1:11 say about self-restraint and steadiness?

The phrase "bear with each other" means that any who follow Christ are to tolerate anyone they find irritating. Oh, gals, I fail at this often. And I find that as I age, what I find irritating can change from moment to moment!

For example, my husband is wonderful whistler. One moment I am enjoying Fred's melodic airy song, but two seconds later I can be annoyed by it! Perhaps it is a craving for silence, or a disruption in my concentration, but I have a choice to make. I can say something snippy, or I can bear with his whistling. Many a marriage has been slowly eroded by the sarcasm of a spouse!

Has someone ever complained about you? *Have you ever complained about someone?* I find that when I get irritated with someone, it's easy for me to start complaining about them. Unkind thoughts, such as, "That person is a jerk," or "They will never change" flood my mind. In those moments, I need to choose to bear with the other person.

Paul also reminds us to *"forgive whatever grievances you may have against one another."*

We are imperfect people living in an imperfect world. People will grieve us, hurt us, and irritate us. You and I must choose to graciously and freely forgive those that do. We choose to forgive because the Lord forgave us. Jesus provides the ultimate example of how we are to respond. Our soft response also prevents us from saying and doing things that we must then ask other people to forgive us for! It's so much harder to take back words than it is to train ourselves not to say them.

IT'S SO MUCH HARDER TO TAKE BACK WORDS THAN IT IS TO TRAIN OURSELVES NOT TO SAY THEM.

7. Record Luke 23:34 below. How does it challenge you to forgive?

Reflect Christ in your love for others.

Our last piece of uniform is love. Love is the glue that holds all the other virtues together. 1 Corinthians 13:13 says, *"The greatest of these is love."* I believe our ability to love others starts with our love for God.

When we love God, we are more likely to demonstrate humility, gentleness, patience, forbearance, and forgiveness. But it's not always easy! We need the help of the Holy Spirit. But our loving well is important enough for Jesus to declare in John 13:35, *"By this all men will know that you are my disciples, if you love one another."*

We are part of God's team, wearing God's uniform. But He gives us the freedom to choose if we will reflect Christ positively or negatively. How do you want the world to see Jesus when they look at you? How do your thoughts, words, and actions reflect Him?

Reflect

Spend time today inspecting each part of your Christian uniform.

Exercise

Answer the following questions.

- How well do I treat others, especially if I am irritated by them?
- How humble am I in my estimate of myself?
- How well do I reflect Christ when I am treated harshly?
- Where can I better offer love and forgiveness?

REFLECTIONS FROM YOUR DRESSING ROOM MIRROR

Day 5

"When we put our problems in God's hands, He puts His peace in our hearts."

~Joyce Meyer, Christian speaker and author

Ladies, I'm going to share with you one of my biggest "issues:" my pride in thinking that I can handle my own problems. This is evidenced by my not asking others to pray for me and with me when a problem sprouts up in my life. When I begin to feel emotionally overwhelmed, mentally fatigued, and spiritually cloudy, that's an indicator that I have failed to place my problems in God's hands.

We've been studying this week about our spiritual wardrobe. As we stand in front of the mirror of God's Word, we need to critically and honestly assess what our life reflects to the world around us. We need to exchange our filthy clothing for Christ's clothing. We need to act worthy of the uniform. As we close out this week, let's look at three instructions Paul directs us to fulfill with thankful hearts.

Read Colossians 3:15-17.

Paul's first instruction is to let peace rule.

I like the Message translation of Colossians 3:15: *"Let the peace of Christ keep you in tune with each other, in step with each other. None of this going off and doing your own thing. And cultivate thankfulness."*

1. As peace is to rule our hearts, what do you learn about peace from the following passages of Scripture?

    a. Psalm 34:12–16

b. John 14:27

c. Romans 14:19

d. Galatians 5:22

e. Ephesians 2:14

f. Philippians 4:7, 9

g. Hebrews 12:14

The peace of God is meant to rule our hearts. The word "rule" in verse 15 can be translated "to act as an umpire." Divine peace should help us overcome our doubts, settle our questions, and make choices that don't intentionally hurt others.

2. Think about another significant relationship in your life. where in your life do you need divine peace to help you intentionally reflect Christ?

Paul's second instruction is to let the Word dwell within us.

The Amplified translation of the Bible helps us to understand the fullness of verse 16: *"Let the [spoken] word of Christ have its home within you [dwelling in your heart and mind—permeating every aspect of your being] as you teach [spiritual things] and admonish and train one another with all wisdom, singing psalms and hymns and spiritual songs with thankfulness in your hearts to God."*

God wants full run of our spiritual house! He wants us to be active Christians who seek to know His Word. The New International translation of the Bible adds the word "richly" after "Let the word of Christ dwell in you." Richly means abundantly.

As we study, meditate on, and apply the Word to our life, it begins to permeate every aspect of our being. Let's face it: if we are to "teach and admonish others," you and I need to have the truth of Scripture guiding our heart, mind, and mouth!

3. What is a practical way you can have God's Word dwell (take up residence) in your life daily?

4. How are Christ-followers called to teach and admonish (warn or correct) others?

5. Not only are we to teach and admonish one another, we are to sing to God with grateful hearts. Be prepared to share at your table, one Christian song you really like, and why it encourages you.

Paul's third instruction is to let our words and deeds glorify Jesus.

Paul brings it home in verse 17, when he sets the norm for Christian conduct with the word "whatever."

Sisters, in whatever you do or say, can you truthfully declare, "Every action I take, every word I speak, gives glory to Jesus"? In reflecting on our Mirror Image theme, we must keep in mind that *whatever* we do or say reflects on Christ—and the world is watching.

6. What boundaries can you put in place before you do or say something, to ensure that you represent Christ well? Feel free to jot down a scripture reference you currently find helpful in your daily walk with Him.

7. Who in your life exhibits this kind of self-control? What are some of the ways these people glorify Jesus in their words and actions?

Paul closes out this last instruction with our need to be thankful. We are to interact with others "with gratitude in our hearts to God." We are to do all things while "giving thanks to God the Father through Him."

Thankfulness literally activates our brain, and increases our capacity to be positive and supportive toward others. Gratitude also lowers our stress level. This is key. We are going to experience times that are hard, painful, or unwanted. Giving thanks in these moments helps us to step away from the ledge and look to Christ. Let's commit to living each day with an attitude of gratitude!

8. Make a gratitude list of attributes God's given you that make you unique.

We began this week's study with my asking you to think about God's Word as a three-paneled mirror. Imagine you are this woman standing in front of the mirror. Jesus is tenderly looking back at you. He knows your struggle, He understands your pain, and He desires your obedience. and He stands ready to take your hand, to help you do life. You hear Him say, "Let My peace rule and My Word dwell. Will you allow Me to change your reflection?"

Reflect

Everyday we have an opportunity to assess our wardrobe in front of the dressing room mirror of God's Word. Reflect on Joyce Meyer's quote, "When we put our problems in God's hands, He puts His peace in our hearts."

Exercise

Write a prayer of praise for where God has given you peace—or—write a prayer of where you want to feel peace, so that you can reflect your trust in Christ.

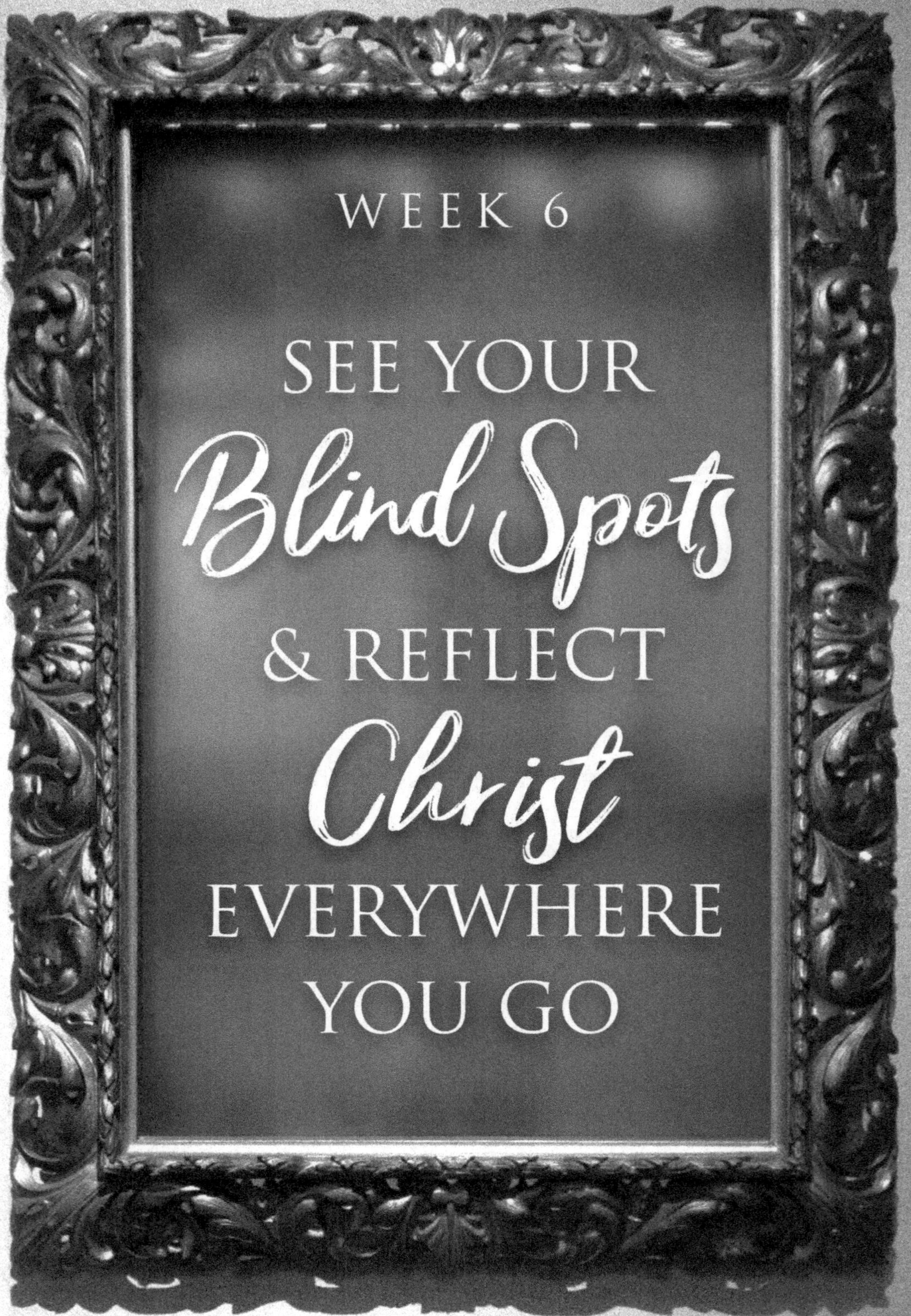

"Jesus who gave sight to the blind can give sight to our blind spots. What if we had the guts to ask Jesus to show us what we refuse to see?"
—Beth Moore

SEE YOUR BLIND SPOTS

Day 1

"Jesus, who gave sight to the blind, can give sight to our blind spots. What if we had the guts to ask Jesus to show us what we refuse to see?"

~Beth Moore, Christian speaker and author

Women who reflect Christ well find the courage to ask Jesus to reveal their blind spots. Blind spots are the moral issues, character flaws, and weaknesses that we have difficulty seeing in ourselves, others, and situations. Just as our car's side-view mirrors help us to compensate for our blind spots while driving, the verses we'll learn this week bring clarity to our relational blind spots.

As I continued to post to social media about mirrors, it dawned on me to ask for thoughts on blind spots in our relationships. Karla responded, offering this great analogy:

> *"When something is in my car's blind spot, my side mirrors flash yellow, alerting me that I'm at risk for lane changes. It's important to surround ourselves with people willing to 'flash yellow' if they see a hazard that we don't. My husband is vital to me with this tactic. It's why our communication is so important."*

As Karla notes, we must be open to feedback from others. In fact, we have to often tell others that they have *our permission* to point out our blind spots, even if it hurts our feelings. When we boldly ask God to reveal our blind spots, He often does so through the people closest to us, because they know us so well.

1. Who on your mental committee has been willing to "flash yellow" for you when they noticed a blind spot? List three names, and how these persons have helped you.

2. Are there people for whom you are willing to "flash yellow"? Jot down three names, and the reason you're willing to take on this role for them. Have they given you permission to do so?

3. God also uses strangers to point out our blind spots, as sometimes it's just emotionally easier for us to hear this feedback from someone that we aren't in close relationship with. Can you think of a time where a stranger helped you to see a blind spot or reevaluate your thinking?

I can so relate to Karla's comment, because my husband is definitely willing to "flash yellow" for me. Fred's understanding of me gives him access to speak wisdom into my life. Gals, I don't just allow it, I *appreciate* it, because I *need* it to become the woman God wants me to be. But I'm going to be real with you and admit that I don't always *like* what Fred has to say!

Sometimes my heart wants to sin—and enjoy it! I want to fester on a hurt, or be grumpy just because it feels good in that moment. And God knows that some days I frankly just don't want to adult. But I am so grateful that He gave me a godly husband who always wants my best and helps me to develop into my best. That's priceless!

Today, let's talk about how blind spots can affect our marriages. This discussion will be of interest even to you lovely single gals, especially if you're doing all you can to prepare your heart and mind for marriage.

Let's read Colossians 3:18-19.

4. What does verse 18 instruct wives to do?

5. Use a dictionary to define the word "submit."

I believe our society has branded "submit" to be a negative word. Many women take it to mean "I am less than," or "My wants and needs must take a back seat to my husband's." I've also heard women say, "Submitting means I become my husband's doormat." Ladies, that's wrong on all counts, even if our men think it's true. That's certainly not the way God views submission, as we'll see from today's readings.

6. Using the following verses, who is the basis of our submission?

   a. Job 22:21

   b. James 4:7

   c. 1 Peter 5:6

7. Now read Luke 2:51. How did Jesus submit to others?

8. How did Jesus demonstrate submission in Luke 22:42?

Matthew 26:39 describes Jesus falling on His face to pray that His Father would provide Jesus with an out to skip the horrors of crucifixion. Jesus understood the hostility and pain He would endure, yet still *chose* obedient submission when God said no. Hebrews 5:8 acknowledges Jesus as God's Son, who "learned obedience from what he suffered." Philippians 3:8 says, "*He became obedient to death—even death on a cross.*"

9. By His example Jesus teaches us that submission isn't always easy, but it brings us into alignment with God's will. How did God honor Jesus' obedience? Record what the following Scriptures tell you.

    a. Philippians 2:9-11

    b. Hebrews 5:9-10

Out of an overflow of our love and appreciation for Christ's submission, we also should choose to follow His example. What are the two greatest commandments? We are to love God, and love others. Both require our submission and death to our selfish desires. Ephesians 5:21 reminds us that believers are to "Submit to one another out of reverence for Christ."

10. What do you learn about submission from the following verses?

    a. Romans 13:1

    b. 1 Peter 2:13-14

    c. Ephesians 5:22

    d. 1 Peter 3:1-6

The closer we draw to Christ, the more we love Him. This makes us better able to love others. I've seen this in marriage, over and over. Fred and I love encouraging couples in their marriages. When we do so, we often refer to the "Marriage Triangle."

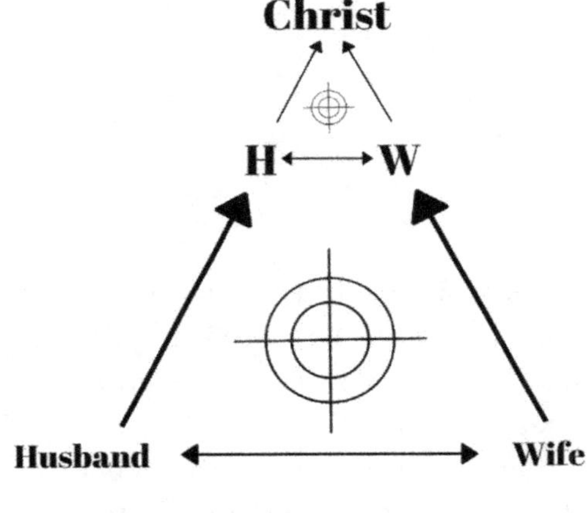

As you can see in this diagram, when a husband and wife each seek to deepen their relationship with Christ, they grow closer to Him. As they grow closer to Christ, they also grow closer to each other.

When conflicts arise, and they will, the marriage relationship becomes a target for the enemy to attack. But the husband and wife who seek unity in Christ present a much smaller target for the devil. There are times when one spouse is closer to Christ than the other is. But even one spouse drawing closer to Christ makes the target smaller! These principles also work with other relationships.

11. Think about your own spouse or significant other. Are you both drawing close to God at the moment? If not, jot down why. Is there anything you can do about this?

As an independent woman, I am still learning what it means to be a submitted wife. My submission to Fred doesn't make me inferior, or less than him. It shows my trust in God's divine plan. Submission requires me to intentionally yield my wants, needs, and desire for control, and place my trust in Fred's leadership. It means believing that even when Fred might struggle to lead well, I trust that God still holds us secure. That's a whole lot of trust right there, ladies! But I can tell you that it works because Fred is a man after God's heart.

My three simple guidelines for yielding to Fred's leadership:

Is it ethical?

Is it moral?

Is it legal?

God calls me to first submit to Him—and then to Fred. And Fred understands and accepts this. So, if Fred were ever to lead our family to make unethical, immoral, or illegal choices, I have *the right* and responsibility to say, "No." There is so much freedom in that!

Yielding in my marriage has given Fred the space to develop into a great leader for our family. That has made a huge difference in our marriage over the years. When I think on the early years of marriage, *when I tried to micromanage every decision Fred tried to make,* I can clearly recall the constant tension in our household. It sure wasn't "home, sweet home" back then! How could it be, when I offered Fred no peace?

Ladies, I still have to daily commit to letting Fred lead, as God made me with such a strong, independent nature. But here is the honest-to-God truth: as I have chosen biblical submission, God has granted me peace, comfort, and joy. All three guard my heart and mind in Christ Jesus, which gets reflected in my countenance.

12. Take a moment and consider how much submission you show your husband (or the man you're dating). Rate yourself on a scale of 1 to 10, with 10 being the most committed to allowing your significant other to hold his position of authority.

13. Now jot down the reasons for the score you gave yourself. If it's low, is it because you've developed the habit of taking the lead? Or is it because your significant other lacks leadership skills, or is not a committed Christian with a right view of submission?

14. In Colossians 3:19, what are husbands instructed to do?

Paul's writings are clear about God's expectations for husbands. A Christian husband is to love his wife, be willing to sacrifice for her, make her wellbeing of primary importance, and care for her as he cares for his own body. A Christ-honoring husband is willing to put aside his own interests to care for his wife. But he won't abuse his leadership role; he understands his words and actions should honor and please God.

In responding to my social post, Terry echoed this point by describing his attitude toward his wife:

> *"Our relationship is stronger and deeper as I'm meeting her needs, bringing her joy, and minimizing her angst, at least the angst I cause. Accomplishing this is an active part of my life and something I strive for daily. I gain great joy by being successful in meeting her needs. And I sense God honoring my desire in this labor of love."*

Isn't that sweet?! He's a keeper! And I'm betting that his wife makes it easy for him to love her well. I'm also betting that she honors him back through her submission. Ladies, we have to become very aware of when our desire for control creates drama and hurt that doesn't need to be there.

Kristy shared this comment about her spouse, in response to my social media post:

> "My relational blind spot with my spouse would be ignoring his feelings and not realizing it. Just because he's a man doesn't mean he doesn't have real feelings. Sometimes he feels that he's just here to pay for my and our kid's whims. Not a great feeling when you realize you're the one that made him feel that way!"

Reflect

How does knowing that biblical submission actually blesses your relationship encourage you to pursue submission God's way?

Exercise

Spend a moment honoring your significant other. Jot down three examples of how your guy has been intentional in honoring you through his leadership. And here's your additional homework: Share your examples with him. Trust me, our men don't hear enough what and when they're doing right!

SEE YOUR BLIND SPOTS

Day 2

"Parents are traffic signs that are always in our blind spots."

~Jeremy

Knowing what traffic signs mean is our first step in obeying them. Traffic signs tell us the suggested speed, what lanes we can use, when we must yield, and perhaps most importantly, when we must stop. Did you know that there are more than 500 federally approved traffic signs in use in our society today?

Traffic signs share a single goal: keep us safe. Today, let's ask God to bring sight to any blind spots we might have in our parent/child relationships.

As I think back to my childhood, I can relate to what Jeremy is saying. As a young child it felt like all I ever heard from my parents was, "Stop that!" or "You're going the wrong way!"

As a teen, it seemed ALL my parents did was post "Road closed!" signs on all the fun I wanted to have. So I started acting like I didn't hear their warnings. I treated my parents like traffic signs in my blind spots. I reasoned that if I didn't pay attention to them, I didn't have to obey them. I was set on doing what I wanted to do, and I didn't really care what God's Word said about it.

Now that I am a parent myself, I know that my defiance hurt God's heart. Scripture is *very clear* on how we are to view our parents and their authority.

1. Write out the following verses, which direct youth on how to act toward their parents.

    a. Exodus 20:12

    b. Deuteronomy 27:16

    c. Proverbs 6:20

    d. Proverbs 23:22

    e. Ephesians 6:1-3

Now read Colossians 3:20-21.

2. What do these verses instruct children to do?

The words honor and obey are repeated over and over in Scripture. Children are to honor their parents and obey them, *no ifs, ands,* or *buts.* The verb obey means to "listen, hear, and heed." When children hear and heed instructions, they please the Lord.

But parents do need to recognize that in a child's developing brain, obedience can be a huge blind spot. Children are making connections, constantly learning, and still developing an awareness of the environment around them. Children might also develop blind spots where they experience trauma.

BUT PARENTS DO NEED TO RECOGNIZE THAT IN A CHILD'S DEVELOPING BRAIN, OBEDIENCE CAN BE A HUGE BLIND SPOT.

I have a vague recollection of my parents divorcing when I was just two. I know this sounds odd, but the stress of that upheaval made it a struggle for me to obey in one specific area: what I chose to eat.

When my dad remarried when I was three, my step-mom, Annie, made many meals that I did not appreciate. I threw food under the table. I hid small bits of food under the edge of my plate. I even hid half-eaten sandwiches in the corners of rooms or in my bedroom closet!

Being caught meant I had to face consequences. These included having to remain at the dinner table until I had eaten my food, standing in the corner where I had tried to hide my food, or cleaning out my bedroom closet. I'm sure Annie was ready to throw in the towel. But she didn't!

I am so thankful that she recognized my trauma and persevered in helping me to process through it. I can only imagine how difficult it must have been to be a new wife, an instant mom to a 3-year-old and a 6-year-old, one of whom (me!) was willfully choosing to be disobedient. Annie's willingness to patiently call me to obedience has cultivated a huge desire within me to honor her as I've aged.

3. As a child, did you struggle with disobedience? How did your parents react? Can you see how their handling of your lack of submission affects how you view your relationships with others today?

4. Are you able to honor your parents now that you're an adult? Has having your own kids opened your eyes to any challenges your parents experienced with you?

Consider the wise words of Kristy Sutton, my friend and author of the blog, *This Hard Calling*: "A child who does not trust an adult will struggle to obey that adult. We need to cultivate trusted relationships built on connection, attachment, and met needs. Fear or forced obedience is not a long-term parenting solution."

Balance that with wisdom from evangelist Billy Graham: "A child who is allowed to be disrespectful to his parents, will not have true respect for anyone else."

As my own two sons have grown and matured, I have often said that parenting isn't for wimps! It's a balancing act made significantly easier by following God's wise counsel. I think one reason God blesses us with children is to further teach us about our blind spots. Too often we default to parenting like we were parented, even when that model wasn't healthy or biblical.

5. What do these verses teach us about training our children in the way they should go?

    a. Psalm 139:13-16

    b. Proverbs 22:6

    c. Matthew 18:1-5

    d. Mark 10:13-16

e. Hebrews 12:7-11

We are called to see the value God sees in our children, as they are made in God's image. We are to train them in the ways of the Lord, providing the needed discipline to produce right living. Discipline must always follow grace, echoing the compassion and love that God shows us as our Heavenly Father. We create discord with our kids when we don't discipline them using the right perspective.

Colossians 3:21, for example, says, "Fathers, do not embitter your children, or they will become discouraged." Other translations use the word provoke in place of embitter. Paul uses the Greek verb *erethizō*, which means to repeatedly "stir up, excite, stimulate or provoke."[1]

How we speak to our kids matters! Especially if God has given us sensitive kids who are easily hurt by our words.

6. Look up the words "provoke" and "discouraged" in your dictionary and record the definitions below.

7. Is God nudging you on how you might be provoking your children? If so, write down these nudgings so that you can talk to God about them during your quiet time.

I think one of the primary ways that Fred and I have provoked our children is through inconsistency. There have been times when we were definitely not on the same page. I would say that something they wanted to do was fine, but Fred would say it wasn't. Sometimes we established boundaries for our boys, but then didn't follow through on the consequences of their disobeying.

Some parents provoke their children by allowing a behavior at home, but then scold them for doing it in public. Other parents are inconsiderate of their child's feelings, insisting that certain emotions be ignored or hidden. Some parents make unreasonable demands or use humiliation to control their child. Look around at all the sullen, withdrawn kids who don't talk to their parents, and you'll see the kids who don't feel safe to be themselves. The kids who don't believe in their God-given value, because that worth has not been reflected to them by their parents.

8. If you are a parent, where do you struggle with being consistent? Where do you struggle with being emotionally honest and present and respectful with your kids?

God wants to be magnified in our parent/child relationships. He wants to be honored in our homes. We are called to yield to the Lord, to treat our children with care, to lovingly discipline them, and to care for their needs. He calls us to firmly establish their steps on a godly path, not create worthiness issues that they'll carry into their teens and adult years.

Parenting is soooo hard, ladies. But parenting can also be incredibly delightful and rewarding. God places these individuals in our care to mold and shape, for His glory. He knows that there will be moments where we'll mess up, but He trusts that we'll do our best to love them just as He loves us. Amazing! Let's become worthy of that trust!

Reflect

Have you given your kids permission to point out what they perceive to be your blind spots? Consider having this discussion. The genius of the conversation, of course, is that in return, your kids have to give you permission to point out theirs! #score

Exercise

Open your Bible. Find and memorize Scripture that specifically speak on parent/child relationships. Tip: there are a lot of them in Proverbs!

SEE YOUR BLIND SPOTS

Day 3

"There are talented people who don't recognize that an underlying attitude or subtle behavior is hurting them and holding them back. Simply put, they just don't see the problem."

~Sara Canaday, Author

Yesterday we talked about parenting, and how important it is that we discipline with grace and love. This is important because when we mess up, our kids can internalize messages that hinder their ability to view themselves as God does.

In her quote above, Sara references the mental baggage that we sometimes start carting around during our childhoods, including negative self-talk and unresolved hurts and shame.

Sometimes, however, a child gets the message from his parents that he's superior to others, that he's "special" and gets to act like it. This leads to a whole different set of problems.

Blind spots can damage our work environments because of jealousy, competitiveness, lack of empathy, or other emotions. Today let's focus on reflecting Christ well on the job.

Read Colossians 3:22-4:1

At the time of his writing his letters to the Colossians, slaves were widely used. Viewed as property, these slaves had no rights. Let's look at Paul's teaching about the standard we are to bring to our daily work, whatever our role.

The first blind spot Paul discusses is how we are to submit to authority in our work.

Paul instructs slaves to "obey your earthly masters in everything." Paul uses the same Greek word that he uses in directing children to obey their parents.

While today we typically replace "obey" with "follow the work rules" or "adhere to company policy," because we have bosses, not masters, God expects us to submit to their authority. I know that some of you are bristling at this idea if you have a terrible boss, but stick with me.

God works for our good. Everything He asks us to do serves to bring Him honor.

1. In verse 22, when are slaves to fulfill Paul's instructions to obey?

Paul's when and how for obedience bring light to blind spots in our submission to authority. Are we fully adhering to our employer's rules, or just enough to not get fired? Are we cooperating only when our bosses are watching? Or are we putting forth our best effort, as working for the Lord, not for man?

2. What does verse 22 say about how are slaves to obey?

3. Look up the word "sincerity" in a dictionary and write the definition below.

When we are sincere, we are genuine in our motives and actions. As Christians, we should genuinely desire to excel in our work. Not just to reap earthly benefits, but to be a crystal clear reflection of Christ's character. Our work ethic speaks volumes about our commitment to God.

The second blind spot Paul addresses is our diligence.

4. Look up the word "diligence" in the dictionary and write the definition below.

5. Colossians 3:23 is one of my favorite verses to quote when I find myself lacking diligence. Look up this verse and write it below.

6. What do we learn about work from the following Scripture?

    a. Genesis 2:15

    b. Psalm 90:17

    c. Proverbs 31:13-17

    d. John 5:17

    e. John 17:4

    f. 1 Corinthians 3:13-14

    g. Titus 2:4-5

God has ordained that we keep our hands busy. If we are going to live out Paul's directive of "work at it with all your heart," we need to bring our best to the work God chooses to give us. We need to work with vigor, cheerfulness, enthusiasm, and diligence, because it pleases Him that we are willing to do so.

WHEN WE APPROACH OUR WORK WITH WHOLEHEARTED EFFORT, WE CULTIVATE AN ATTITUDE OF "I GET TO," RATHER THAN AN ATTITUDE OF "I HAVE TO."

When we approach our work with wholehearted effort, we cultivate an attitude of "I get to," rather than an attitude of "I have to." When we see our work as opportunities to be difference makers in God's Kingdom, we can cease to view it as drudgery.

7. How is your work ethic in these areas? Can you say that you reflect Christ well in each?

    a. At home

    b. At the office

    c. At the church

    d. Other

The third blind spot Paul highlights is our motivation.

I am motivated by rewards and recognition, likely because of my achiever personality. But if I am not keeping my eyes on God, I can fall to the temptation of craving and even needing external rewards to be motivated to work. I'm talking about the dangling carrot of reward and public kudos that spur me forward. *Can you relate?*

But what happens when there is no carrot? What happens when our work hard is overlooked? What happens when our coworker gets the promotion we feel we deserve? Does God give us an "out" to not continue to bring our best? Sorry, no.

My carrots, for years, were award certificates and trophies. I was motivated by the opportunity to receive them and display them on my shelves. Ladies, I was so proud of these "validations" of my worth that they became idols to me. I wanted more. I needed more!

I am NOT saying that award certificates and trophies are bad, gals, so please don't rush home and hide any you have on display. These accolades only become an issue *when they become a heart issue*, and affect how we view ourselves and our place in the world.

I always chuckle when I hear a story of some celebrity or politician not getting her way and screaming, "DO YOU KNOW WHO I AM?" (Lol. Yes, we know you're a brat.)

8. What does Matthew 6:19 say happens to the things we treasure here on earth?

Matthew 6:20 goes on to say that we should, instead, store up treasures in heaven, where rust and moth can't destroy. Our real motive should be an imperishable reward that has heavenly value.

9. What, per Colossians 3:24, will Christian workers receive from God?

Paul says we work for earthly masters, but the Lord is in charge of our reward. When we serve those in authority over us well, we serve Christ well. When we are faithful with the work of our hands, God notices. Our salvation is secured through Christ, but we will receive heavenly rewards based on our good works.

10. What do you learn about the rewards God gives Christians from 2 Corinthians 5:10?

Reflect

Think about your own obedience, diligence, and motivation in the work place. What are some specific examples of how you have worked for the Lord, rather than man?

Exercise

Record any changes in your attitude toward work that you feel God is prompting you to make to better reflect Christ.

REFLECT CHRIST EVERYWHERE YOU GO

Day 4

"God will use you for great things on the condition that you believe much more in Him than your own weakness."

~Mother Teresa

I love this quote, in part because I am amazed at how selfless Mother Teresa was. Talk about ceaselessly working for the Lord 24/7!

My friend Beth shared this quote when she delivered a message titled "Beautiful You" at a retreat we both attended. As I listened to Beth be so vulnerable in her struggles with self-image, weight, and worthiness, I found myself agreeing with her that our negative thoughts about ourselves might be our greatest weakness.

Beth shared that from childhood, she had fully internalized the message that she was unattractive, even though it wasn't true. "I started dieting at eleven years old," she shared, "I thought I was so overweight. But when I look back at old photos, I realize that what I saw in the mirror as a teenager came from what I *perceived* to be true."

Gals, I wanted to dig deeper into this idea of our own negative thoughts being our greatest weakness. On Facebook I asked women to share the lies that bombard their minds when they see their reflection.

Valerie shared that she often hears the lie that she's not good enough. "My mind wanders back to when I was a shy, quiet little girl at school," she wrote. "I wasn't popular, and was typically picked last for P.E."

Katie shared about feeling super self-conscious. "When I look in the mirror," she wrote, "I see the unflattering physical traits of a chromosome deficiency. These traits leave me not liking my looks, even though I know I am beautifully and wonderfully made by God. I work hard daily to remember whose I am. I tell myself that I am just as He wanted me to be for His plan."

1. Can you relate to these struggles? When you look in the mirror, do you still think thoughts planted in your childhood? Jot down one thought below that still has the power to make you self-conscious.

The hard part is that we can't get away from mirrors. They're everywhere: in our home bathrooms, at our offices, and in every restaurant bathroom. We even catch our reflection in bus windows and reflected in water. If we hate what we see, we walk around with a defeated, negative spirit. When we walk around focused on hating ourselves, we don't do a good job of reflecting the beauty of Christ.

Donna captured this truth in her response to my post. "How it must break His heart," she wrote, "to hear me hate how He made me. I'm slowly learning to approach a mirror and hear God say to me, 'If only you could see yourself through My eyes.'"

Like mirrors, our lives reflect how we perceive our value. We might think we're doing a good job of hiding our insecurities, but they still leak out. We will NEVER be able to live up to society's standard of perfection, so I have to ask the obvious question: *Why do we think we need to try?*

Pam shared this insight with me: "Even though I know I'm not perfect and never can be, I still strive for perfection." When I read that, I immediately asked her why. Her response: "I feel that we have a lot of pressure from society and the media to always look and be our best. I have to remind myself when I look in a mirror that I am who He has made me to be and I will ALWAYS be perfect in His sight!!!"

The challenge with our appreciation of beauty is that it is subjective. You might think Tom Cruise is cute, but your friend thinks he's a toad. (Sorry, Tom!) You might be attracted to bald men, and your friend won't date one. You might like tall, dark, and handsome, but your friend thinks beefy blondes rock the world.

The mirror reflects our thoughts, ladies, not reality. You think mirrors make you look fat—which makes all of your friends want to kick your size 2 butt! But even thin, gorgeous models are highly critical of themselves, which just proves that reality is all in our head! Our thoughts are powerful.

Thoughts established in childhood have power.

Barbara wrote, "I do what I can to enhance the best me God has made. I was most fortunate to have had family and parents who instilled in me such positive thoughts that I don't often think negative thoughts of myself."

Barbara is most fortunate indeed. What is said to us as children sets the course of our thinking into adulthood. For the moms reading this, let's all commit to speaking words of life to our children so they have to fight fewer battles for their self-image.

Thoughts repeated over and over throughout our life have power.

Darty shared, "Even after losing 90+ pounds, and keeping it off for over five years, I still see a fat girl looking back at me. I guess being that girl for 35 years makes it hard to erase the image."

Though she has shed the pounds she wanted to lose, Darty is still carrying a heavy load.

Thoughts about our what ifs have power.

Kristy shared, "I think more soul stuff when I see my reflection. Things like "What if people really knew you" and "You failed again!" Kristy continued, "I was talking to my small group last week about the enemy's assault on femininity and womanhood. It's so healing to just go to those hard spaces and ask why we believe what we do. I'm learning to break agreements I made in the past with any lies big or small that have been spewed in my direction."

I love that we don't have to ask what if with God. He already knows everything about us and still chooses to love us!

Ladies, if we want to go from disliking ourselves to being women who are confident in how God made us, then our thoughts matter! What peace and power would we enjoy, if every time we saw our reflection we saw these words instead of our flaws?

2. Take time now to write this sentence five times. Each time, ask God to anchor the truth that He says you are beautiful apart from your appearance. Also write the sentences on index cards and post them on your fridge, your bathroom mirror, your car visor, and any other high-traffic area where you will see them often. Read the words aloud and watch God move!

3. Look up the below verses and write them out in the space provided. Which ones speak to you? Put those verses on index cards and say them aloud every time you see them. Get ready for your life to change!

    a. Joshua 1:9

    b. Psalm 34:5

    c. Psalm 46:5

    d. Proverbs 3:15

    e. Proverbs 31:25

    f. Proverbs 31:30

g. Song of Solomon 4:7

h. Luke 1:45

i. 1 Peter 3:3-4

We can change the way we think about our reflection. No matter where we are we have opportunity to best reflect Christ. Ladies, don't we want our reflection to be a mirror-image of Christ? When we choose to view ourselves with the worth God places in us, we truly radiate an unfading beauty. Could that be answer to the age-old pursuit of the fountain of youth?

I was pondering this idea of the fountain of youth when I read Juli's response to my social media post. "My fine lines and wrinkles are truly nothing more than proof that I've been blessed with a life longer than some. The condition of my soul is what God cares about most. When my relationship with Him is healthy, others will see Him and His beauty through me. They can't help but overlook what I think are flaws."

I'm not gonna lie: I spend a lot of time trying to look great for my husband. In part because he loves taking photos of me. I love that he delights in my appearance. I *do* sometimes focus on my crow's feet, but I know that his love for me is secure because he fully loves my heart.

God also cares most about the condition of our heart. Developing a healthy relationship with Him includes overcoming our "self" focused tendencies that tarnish our reflection of Him.

Self-focused tendencies such as...
Self-esteem
Self-sufficiency
Self-talk
Self-care

4. It is crazy how much our world emphasizes "self." What other self phrases can you think of?

Reflect

- Let's trade pursuing a better self-esteem, for pursuing God-esteem.
- Let's trade craving self-sufficiency for God-sufficiency.
- Let's trade our self-talk for God-talk taken straight from scripture.
- Let's trade our emphasis on self-care for an emphasis on our spiritual-care.

Exercise

Choose one of the trades above to focus on this week.

REFLECT CHRIST EVERYWHERE YOU GO

Day 5

*"The Lord does not look at the things people look at.
People look at the outward appearance, but the Lord looks at the heart."*

1 Samuel 16:7

If we are going to win the battle against the constant attack on our self-image, we need to care far more about our hearts than we do about our looks. We need to be women who know the standard we should be reflecting.

We belong to Jesus Christ and we are created to be a reflection of Him!

> WE BELONG TO JESUS CHRIST AND WE ARE CREATED TO BE A REFLECTION OF HIM!

As we complete this study, my desire is that these truths are now anchored in your mind. My prayer is that when you look at your reflection in any mirror, you see Jesus looking back at you, with unconditional love! My encouragement is that you choose to embrace reflecting Christ well to help others to gain freedom from the pressure of trying to live up to society's skewed of self and perfection.

Let us look at Paul's important final instructions to the Colossians.

Read Colossians 4:2-4:4.

Paul instructs the Colossian believers to be devoted to prayer.

The word devote means to dedicate one's time, attention, and strength to a task. Paul set the example of devotion to prayer. Look again at Colossians 1:9-12. What is Paul continually praying for the Colossians?

Prayer is about talking with God. Conversation is essential for the health of our relationships, right? The question we need to ask ourselves is, "Do I value prayer as my means of communicating with God?"

Our salvation is much more than what some call a "fire insurance policy." Being saved isn't just about escaping hell and being assured of heaven. While we are still living our lives on earth, God longs for a close, intimate relationship each of us. Pause and take a quick assessment of your communication with God. How often do you pray? What do you pray about? Do you pray mostly when you need something?

1. How does Paul tell us to pray in 1 Thessalonians 5:17-18?

2. As we devote ourselves to pray, we are to be both watchful and thankful. Look up the word watchful in your dictionary and write it below. Why is it important to pray with a watchful attitude?

3. What do you learn about the need for watchful praying from Matthew 26:41 and 1 Corinthians 10:12-13?

Paul wants us to avoid spiritual defeat because he knows that Satan is like a roaring lion looking for someone to devour. We need to be in constant communication with God, through prayer, to successfully navigate life's ups and downs. We also need to pray for others. I remind myself often that it is better to talk to God about people, *than it is to talk about people to people.*

In my own prayer life, I've found it helpful to keep a weekly prayer calendar and daily prayer journal. My prayer calendar helps me to remember to pray each day for specific people. I jot brief notes by each name, as God answers my prayers.

In my prayer journal, I write out my response to time spent in God's word, recording what He is doing in my life and the lives of those for whom I am praying. I also journal more specific requests based on needs I see, and what is happening in my life. As I have prayed for my husband over the years, I've been able to write many prayers of thanksgiving in my prayer journal for how God has worked in his life.

You may find it helpful to view the sample prayer calendar available on my website at https://elizabethmahusay.com/resources.

Read Colossians 4:5-6.

Paul instructs the believers to be wise and purposeful.

We are to be wise in the way we act toward non-believers, as they are always watching how we live.

4. Record some truths you gain about being wise from the following passages.

    a. Proverbs 3:7, 16:3

    b. Isaiah 29:14

    c. Daniel 12:3

    d. 1 Corinthians 1:25

    e. 2 Timothy 3:15

f. James 3:13

Each day we are called to consistently live by the truth from God's Word, and to purposefully look for opportunities to share the Gospel. How we share the Gospel matters. The perceived exclusivity of the Gospel is offensive to many in our modern culture, but our delivery of the Good News should not be.

We've all seen those megaphone Christians that make us cringe, right? The ones who stand on street corners and yell that sinner are going to hell. Granted, salvation is necessary, but yelling at people in a judgmental tone only works with a low percentage of "sinners." (There are some people who only respond out of fear.)

Let us, instead, share the hope of Christ graciously and with respect. Our goal is to walk in such a way, and talk in such a way, that people give us opportunities to tell them about Christ. Be willing to follow the Holy Spirit's leading, so that you are able to share the Gospel message in a way the person will be open to.

I've shared the Gospel on a napkin, by drawing three circles on a board, and by using objects on my restaurant table! What's a unique way you've heard or seen the Gospel presented? Share in your small group.

Read Colossians 4:7-18.

Paul's last instruction is for the believers to faithfully work.

5. Paul acknowledges the faithful comfort and encouragement of believers in his inner circle. In verses 7-11, how does Paul describe these companions?

6. What do you learn about the work of the following people? I've provided supporting Scriptures you can use to gain even more details.

   a. Tychicus (See 2 Timothy 4:12 and Titus 3:12)

b. Onesimus (See Philemon 10-12)

c. Aristarchus (See Acts 19:28-41)

d. Epaphras

e. Luke

f. Archippus

7. Which of the above individuals do you most identify with, and why?

In this season of my life I most identify with Epaphras, because he wrestled in prayer on behalf of others. I find myself asking God to help my two sons to "stand firm in all the will of God, mature and fully assured." As they transition into adulthood and face the challenges that brings, I wrestle in prayer over my desire to control things. But I need to instead trust that God has a perfect plan for each them! *Can you relate with your own children?*

8. Describe a situation over which you've wrestled in prayer. Has there been an outcome?

Paul challenges our faith and calls us to be devoted in prayer, watching for opportunities to reflect Christ. We are called to be wise and purposeful in our interactions, so that we can make the most of every opportunity to share Christ. We are called to faithfully work, so that we are an encouragement to our Christian brothers and sisters as we seek to advance the Kingdom of God.

9. Think of at least one Christian that you can encourage. How and when will you do so?

Reflect

Think about a recent conversation you had. Was it full of grace and seasoned with salt? Colossians 4:6.

Exercise

Who can you be more purposeful in sharing the Gospel with this week? Pray that God helps you to develop a plan to do so, based on their personality, interests, and needs.

"Let's be women committed to living a life that reflects Christ."
—Elizabeth

CLOSING REFLECTIONS

Ladies, we did it! We walked through a study of Colossians. My prayer is that you've found space on the pages of this study to be completely honest before God, and that our time together has brought transformation to your character.

Digging into the Word of God will help you to clearly reflect Christ. So please keep growing in your knowledge of the Bible. You can deepen what you've learned in this study by walking through it a second time with your friends. You can always purchase additional copies of the book on my website.

2 Corinthians 3:18 is such an encouragement on our journey to becoming more Christ-like in our reflections: "And we, who with unveiled faces all reflect the Lord's glory, are being transformed into His likeness with ever-increasing glory, which comes from the Lord, who is the Spirit."

As Oswald Chambers once noted,

> "The greatest characteristic a Christian can exhibit is this completely unveiled openness before God, which allows that person's life to become a mirror for others. When the Spirit fills us, we are transformed, and by beholding God we become mirrors. You can always tell when someone has been beholding the glory of the Lord, because your inner spirit senses that she mirrors the Lord's own character. Beware of anything that would spot or tarnish that mirror in you."

In Exodus 34, Moses fixed his eyes on the glory of God while on Mount Sinai. When he came down, carrying the tablets of stone, his face was radiant. Seeing Moses, the Israelites were afraid to come near him. So Moses placed a veil over his face in the presence of the people. Imagine spending so much time in God's presence that your face radiates, too!

Paul urges us, in Romans 12:1-2 to present our bodies as a living sacrifice, and to not conform to the pattern of the world, but be transformed by the renewing of our minds. We are to die to our old way of life so that we reflect Christ.

When we are saturated with the presence of the Lord, we no longer conform to the world's way of thinking and living.

WHEN WE ARE SATURATED WITH THE PRESENCE OF THE LORD, WE NO LONGER CONFORM TO THE WORLD'S WAY OF THINKING AND LIVING.

We choose to step in front of the full-length mirror of God's Word and allow the truth to magnify our wrong thinking and wrong living. We willingly die to self and aim to be crystal clear in our Christianity. We renew our minds because we know that transformation in our thinking leads to transformation in our living.

We continually inspect our reflection of Christ, looking for distortions that need to be removed. We rely on the whole counsel of the Word of God to be our dressing room mirror as we clothe ourselves in our custom-labeled uniform. We actively look for and address our relational blind spots so that we can reflect Christ everywhere we go!

The result is our ability to "test and approve what God's will is." That excites me because at the end of the day I want to know and do "His good, pleasing and perfect will." I can confidently tell you that His will is for us to be a mirror images of Christ. We can break the chains of comparison that imprison us and confidently walk in the freedom that we are created in His image!

Precious sisters, I leave you with these wise words from David Wilkerson:

"If I am not Christ-like at heart—if I'm not becoming noticeably more like Him—then I have totally missed God's purpose for my life. It doesn't matter what I accomplish for His kingdom. If I miss this one purpose, I have lived, preached, and yes, striven in vain. God's purpose is fulfilled in me only by what I am becoming in Him. Christ-likeness isn't about what I do for the Lord, but about how I'm being transformed into His likeness."

Yes Lord! May our heart's desire be that we are transformed into a Mirror Image of You!

Reflect

How has your understanding of who you are in Christ been affected by this study?

How has the study challenged you in:

- your prayer life?
- your thought life?
- sharing your faith?
- how you view mirrors?

Write a prayer of commitment for how you plan to live a life that reflects Christ.

ENDNOTES

Chapter 1

1 Walvoord, John F. and Zuck, Roy B. The Bible Knowledge Commentary, New Testament Edition. Cook Communications Ministries, 2004. Pages 668, 669

2 McDowell, Josh. "The Bible Is Unique." *Josh.org*, 2011, www.josh.org/resources/apologetics/videos/.

3 *Blue Letter Bible*, 2020, www.blueletterbible.org/kjv/col/1/1/t_conc_1108011.

4 "G5281 - Hypomonē - Strong's Greek Lexicon (KJV)." *Blue Letter Bible*, 2020, www.blueletterbible.org/lang/lexicon/lexicon.cfm?Strongs=G5281&t=KJV.

5 "G3115 - Makrothymia - Strong's Greek Lexicon (KJV)." *Blue Letter Bible*, 2020, www.blueletterbible.org/lang/lexicon/lexicon.cfm?Strongs=G3115&t=KJV.

Chapter 2

1 "G4138 - Plērōma - Strong's Greek Lexicon (KJV)." *Blue Letter Bible*, 2020, www.blueletterbible.org/lang/lexicon/lexicon.cfm?Strongs=G4138&t=KJV.

2 "Ambassador, Ambassage - Vine's Expository Dictionary of New Testament Words." *Blue Letter Bible*, 2020, www.blueletterbible.org/search/Dictionary/viewTopic.cfm?topic=VT0000107.

3 "G4137 - Plēroō - Strong's Greek Lexicon (KJV)." *Blue Letter Bible*, 2020, www.blueletterbible.org/lang/lexicon/lexicon.cfm?Strongs=G4137&t=KJV.

Chapter 3

1 Meyer, Joyce. *Battlefield of the Mind: How to Win the War in Your Mind.* Time Warner, 1995.

2 "G3880 - Paralambanō - Strong's Greek Lexicon (KJV)." *Blue Letter Bible*, 2020, www.blueletterbible.org/lang/lexicon/lexicon.cfm?Strongs=G3880&t=KJV.

3 "G3884 - Paralogizomai - Strong's Greek Lexicon (KJV)." *Blue Letter Bible*, 2020, www.blueletterbible.org/lang/lexicon/lexicon.cfm?Strongs=G3884&t=KJV.

4 "Facts & Figures." *Facts & Figures | Chicken Soup for the Soul*, 16 Sept. 2013, www.chickensoup.com/about/facts-and-figures.

Chapter 6

1 "G2042 - Erethizō - Strong's Greek Lexicon (KJV)." *Blue Letter Bible*, 2020, www.blueletterbible.org/lang/lexicon/lexicon.cfm?Strongs=G2042&t=KJV.

ABOUT THE AUTHOR

A seasoned women's Bible study writer and teacher, Elizabeth enjoys engaging women through God's Word. She is the author of Transform My Thinking, God and has written several other Bible studies including Joshua, Ecclesiastes, prayer, and a study equipping women who desire to lead studies. She is Women's Minister of Cottonwood Creek Church and the founder of Bible Reading Diehards, a group designed to encourage reading the Bible daily and completely in a year.

Elizabeth graduated with her bachelor's in Chemistry Education and a master's in Instructional Technology from the University of South Florida. She taught high school science for 10 years. Elizabeth married her high school sweetheart, Fred. They have two sons. She has been an entrepreneur for over 18 years and has helped her husband build his flourishing photography business.

More from Elizabeth:

Are your thoughts leading you to live the fulfilling life God wants you to have?

Our daily habits are the direct result of what we tell ourselves.
Are your thoughts influenced by cultural soundbites—
"Just do it!", "You got this!", "It's up to you!"
— or what God says in His Word?

Learn what God says about you through
5 weeks of personal study and 6 teaching videos!

Paperback, eBook, and DVD series available at
ElizabethMahusay.com

Elizabeth and Fred Mahusay have a heart for marriages. Every Monday they host a live broadcast called **Marriage Matters Monday**. Be sure to tune in as they share biblically based marriage encouragement!

Visit and Like the 'Rock My Marriage' Facebook page:
www.facebook.com/rockmymarriage

Made in USA - Kendallville, IN
1079404_9781640858237
04.14.2020 0921